KINDLING
A KINDRED
SPIRIT

KINDLING
A
KINDRED
SPIRIT

A Woman's Guide to
Intimate Christian Friendship

Cheryl M. Smith

CHRISTIAN PUBLICATIONS
CAMP HILL, PENNSYLVANIA

Christian Publications
3825 Hartzdale Drive, Camp Hill, PA 17011

Faithful, biblical publishing since 1883

ISBN: 0-87509-586-0
LOC Catalog Card Number: 95-71781
© 1996 by Christian Publications
All rights reserved
Printed in the United States of America

96 97 98 99 00 5 4 3 2 1

#34771255

Cover art by
Glenda Conklin

Dedicated to my husband, lover and friend Scott

CONTENTS

Preface 1

1. Clearing the Cobwebs 5

2. Killing the Lone Ranger 27

3. Loneliness: Learning to Live 45
   with Transition

4. Love at Arm's Length 67

5. Of a Kindred Spirit 87

6. When It Isn't Working 115

7. Walls, Bridges or Gates? 137

8. The Truth about Risk 161

9. Friendship Close to Home 181

10. Closer Than a Brother 209

11. What Is Christian Love Anyway? 231

12. Jonathan and David 251
    The Power of Friendship

Bibliography 267

Preface

It was December 28th and time to return home. We slid into the orange vinyl seats in the terminal waiting area to meet our final flight home. Weary travelers burdened with evidence of Christmas past surrounded us. For some, like our family, it was a stop en route. For others, it was a time for parting.

A short distance away another group prepared to board their plane. I watched the sea of emotions unfold. Tearful farewells, last embraces, brave smiles and hearty waves signified both an ending as well as an invisible, enduring link between families and friends.

Friendship—it's that warmth of the soul that connects two people. If airport partings are an indicator, friendship is a rather common commodity. Most people have friends. In fact, many people have close friends, that is, a select few with whom they can share their innermost thoughts and feelings. But how many people have intimate friends who might be called "kindred spirits"? By this I mean, friends who are willing to hold us accountable when we need it. Friends who will help us become all God wants us to be.

The more I study the Bible, the more I'm convinced God wants to use friendship in our lives in a beautiful and powerful way. A kindred spirit friend is one who holds a measure of your life in her hand as a sacred trust from God. Yet I'm also convinced that such relationships are increasingly rare. *Kindling a Kindred Spirit* is a biblical look at intimate Christian friendship. It is not only about building kindred spirit relationships between Christians, but also about the kindred Spirit who overshadows the entire process.

Many good books on friendship have been written over the years. Still, I have yet to read one that answers fully and biblically the practical questions raised in this text. How do friendship and ministry mix? Should you keep in touch with friends following a move? Are there ways to soften the sting of loneliness that characterizes that first year of transition? How can you find and develop a kindred spirit friendship? How should a Christian deal with a difficult friendship? Are there limits to the confidences you entrust to a friend? What does Christian love really look like? These have been part of my quest. The answers God has revealed have thrilled and challenged me. I know they will do the same for you.

These biblical insights offer practical counsel for everyday relationships. In addition, the

"Making It Yours" section at the end of each chapter offers questions to guide you in personalizing these insights or to use the book for group discussions.

We all have mental photo albums in our minds. Among the snapshots of pleasant memories are experiences shared with friends. I share some of these memories in *Kindling a Kindred Spirit*. I generally alter the testimonies to protect a person's identity. In this book, however, many names have been left unchanged to honor those whose friendships have warmed my heart and touched my life.

Several such friends deserve additional recognition here. It is through their efforts that this book has come about. My thanks to:

-Teresa Heffner and Pam Hoogestraat, whose encouragement and help in so many ways made this project possible.
-Jackie McCoy for reviewing the book from a counseling perspective.
-David Stickney, and my husband, Scott, for keeping me biblically accurate.
-Beth Cockrel and Mary Webb for keeping me grammatically correct, and for their invaluable encouragement and prayer support.

A special thanks to Pam Taylor for her friendship and editorial expertise.

Kindling a Kindred Spirit is a product of kindred hearts.

Chapter 1

Clearing the Cobwebs

M om, watch this!" Sierra shouted gleefully from the top of the slide at McDonald's Playland. I set down my fizzy Coke and squinted in her direction against the midday sun. Swish! Down the slide she sped. Another preschooler waited at the bottom. They exchanged grins and a few hurried words. Then off they raced to experience it all over again. Sierra had found a playmate. She glowed with happiness, absorbed in the extra fun of shared play.

Not far from me, two young mothers leaned over the crumpled remains of Happy Meals and visited earnestly. The wind caught their words and flung about their laughter. I heard catches of their conversation about a Bible study group, home life and children.

How I envied them, sitting there enjoying each other's company. I remembered the warm comaraderie of women's Bible studies I'd attended in the past. I would have given anything to be part of such a group now. I sighed. *There's no chance of that, now that I'm a pastor's wife,* I thought. *It would be treason to go someplace else to attend a study that would suit my needs, and I sure don't have what it takes to lead one. I wonder, why does life in ministry have to be so terribly lonely?*

"God," I prayed bitterly, "I'd give anything to have lunch with a friend." I did not take the extra step to pray for God to send such a friend to me because I thought it was useless. A pastor's wife should be friendly with everyone, but close to no one, I told myself. Besides, friendship in the church was just too risky. Any pastor's wife could tell you that developing a close friendship with someone in the church would only make others jealous. Hadn't God promised to be enough for me? Where was my faith?

Maybe my self pity was unwarranted. Ministry life was lonely, but God was all I really needed. My relationship with Him would fill the void of friendship in my heart. And, of course, I had my husband and children to relate to. I decided the adjustment to ministry life would just take more time.

The lunch hour had passed. Nearby the two women were busy preparing to leave. I called to Sierra and we also made our way to the parking lot. Yet as Sierra drifted off to sleep in her car seat during the long drive home, my thoughts were dogged by loneliness. I fought off depression with my best rationalizations. Our church didn't seem to hold many prospects for friendship. It doesn't take too long in a congregation of 35 or so to know who's a possibility and who's not. Nearly everyone was much older than me. Their lives seemed too different from mine to touch in a significant way.

"Besides," I reminded myself, "I really don't have time for friendship." I had always been one to keep myself busy. The ministry seemed to demand constant attention and priority. It brought relief from the boredom of my tedious routines at home. If I had been honest, I would have admitted that busyness was also one way I kept loneliness at bay.

We had been at that logging town pastorate in Western Washington only a year. Living there had meant a difficult cultural adjustment. While I was used to the rush of city life, I found myself in a rough-and-tumble, ruggedly independent town of 1,000. Life was slower, more solitary, and the winters were dismally wet and gloomy. Yet moving there also revealed to me many misconceptions I had about friendship in Christian life and ministry.

However, these misconceptions were not mine alone. Many pastors' wives had warned me about the hazards of developing close friendships within the congregation. One told me that she hadn't had a close friendship in over 10 years. Another confided that after four years in ministry, she still didn't have a friend she felt she could really trust. I wasn't surprised by what these women shared and the emotional pain they endured. Loneliness is one of the top complaints of pastors' wives across denominational lines.

But loneliness is experienced by people in other walks of life, too. Talk to people who have come to Christ as adults and they'll tell you that the transition from non-Christian to Christian friendships is often a lonely passage. In fact, one of the biggest challenges in evangelism and church growth is helping people become integrated into their local churches. Fitting into established circles of relationships, even at church, is a difficult challenge for most people.

Within the church walls, relationships should be warmer. We sing: "I'm so glad I'm a part of the family of God . . ." but guilty questions hang in the air even as the pianist plays. Do we really feel a part? Does attending your local church feel like a surrogate family or another social obligation? Who's fault is this loneliness anyway? And why do those in ministry often feel the loneliest of all?

I believe the guilt of loneliness lies at our own doors. Subtle misconceptions crafted by Satan have twisted scriptural teaching regarding friendship. Like dust and cobwebs covering an attic antique, these thoughts sift over our lives and prevent us from enjoying the beauty of friendship as God intended it. Here are a few misconceptions I've uncovered.

M*isconception #1: I don't need close friend-ships. My relationships with God and my family are enough.*

It's hard to believe, but I once thought this was true. As I wrestled with loneliness in our first pastorate, I privately upbraided myself for being so emotionally weak. Hadn't God called us to this town? Hadn't He promised to enable me? I thought if I was struggling, it was only because I was lacking in faith. But while God does promise to meet our needs, He never expects that we live in continuous isolation.

In Genesis 2 God placed Adam in a perfect world. He not only lived at harmony with creation, but his fellowship with God was warm and unbroken by sin. Adam may not have been aware of the relational void in his life, but God was. He said: "It is not good for the man to be alone. I will make a helper suitable for him" (Genesis 2:18). Enter Eve. Eve was God's answer to Adam's aloneness. She was specially created to work beside him, bear his children and share his life. And while Adam's original purpose revolved around work, Eve's role in creation was primarily relational.

It's no wonder then that relational issues are so important to women. We are divinely designed for such concerns. Likewise, it should have been no surprise to me that I was struggling with loneliness following a move that left former friendships far behind. My struggle was not because I lacked spiritual backbone. Rather it was simply that God had designed me for friendship and that need wasn't being filled.

We also need to realize that while our husband and children can fill some of those voids, it is foolish to expect they will fill all of them. In her book *When Lovers Are Friends*, Merle Shain wisely observed:

> We each need several people to unlock all the chambers of our heart. And while we have all been conditioned to hunger for the one person who gives us everything and gives it to us all of the time, it helps to accept that life doesn't consist of total people. (Shain 1978, 102)

Amen. The reference to "total people" includes husbands, too. My husband is probably my closest friend, but I've discovered that trying to make him my only friend overburdens our relationship. Friendships, both those we share as husband and wife and those we don't, bring strength and vitality to our married life.

Misconception #2: Avoiding cliques means giving up close friendships within the church.

As a pastor's wife, I used to feel I should be everyone's friend. I also believed I didn't have the right to close friendships within the congregation. A quick trip through the book of James and it's not hard to see how my misconception got started. James 2:1 begins with a harsh command: "My brothers, as believers in our glorious Lord Jesus Christ, don't show favoritism." Paraphrased in relational terms, this means: Don't just cater to the people you like at church; include the outsider. James goes on to say,

> If you really keep the royal law found in Scripture, "Love your neighbor as yourself," you are doing right. But if you show favoritism, you sin and are convicted by the law as lawbreakers. (James 2:8-9)

In other words, if you are serious about living out Christian friendship, don't leave the newcomer sitting off by himself.

We all know the difficulty of breaking into new social circles. Some years ago when our family began attending a local church, my husband was asked to teach an adult Sunday school class for new Christians. So I went off to find my own class for the hour. Perusing the list of classes offered, I chose the one for my age group.

The first Sunday I arrived a few minutes early, eager to get acquainted with some new people. I was soon disappointed. The teacher introduced himself to me, but no one else spoke a word of welcome. "People are naturally shy," I consoled myself. "Maybe next week I'll get to know someone." Back I went the next Sunday. This time I took the first step and introduced myself. I was given a polite reply and then abandoned as the person went off to talk and sit with her friends. The next week I tried again, with the same results. By the end of the month, I found myself dreading the Sunday school hour. The next Sunday I gave up and changed to another class. This group was friendlier. Over time, I was able to connect a few names with faces. Still, I've noticed on most Sundays those who have known each other over the years quickly cluster together to catch up on the week's happenings, leaving newcomers to brave the icebreaking alone or return home as lonely as they came.

Did these Christians intentionally push me aside? I don't think so. They were simply gravitating toward the people they knew and loved. Besides, Sunday school isn't the best setting for getting acquainted. But James says that Christian friendship should step out of the comfort zone and welcome the newcomer regardless of personal preference.

Compare for a moment this experience with my adjustment to another church situation. Again my husband was busy with ministry involvements elsewhere and I found myself attending a new Sunday school class alone. This was a large class with about 50 to 60 people crowded onto folding chairs each Sunday morning to spend the hour together. "How will I ever get to know anyone in this group?" I worried nervously as I gripped my styrofoam coffee cup and tried to look relaxed.

I needn't have worried. Debbie was at my side in a flash. "You must be new," she said with a big smile. "I'm Debbie. Welcome to our class. . . ." She introduced me to several people and invited me to sit with her when class began. For the next several weeks, while I was getting acquainted, I was her special project. Then one day she explained what I feel is the heart of James 2:1-9. She said, "I hope you don't mind my not visiting with you much on Sunday mornings anymore. I try to make it a priority to reach out to new people during that time. I try to help them feel welcome. I reserve other times for catching up with friends." And so she did. Other times were shared together, but Sunday morning was saved for the newcomer.

We all need times to be with those we know. Jesus Himself took Peter, James and John apart to be with Him while He prayed in the Garden of Gethsemane. This wasn't a time for outreach. Instead it was a time for tried and trusted friends. Does Christian friendship mean we are everyone's buddy? No, it doesn't. But it does mean we are selective about the private times we have with friends. And it means we are available to God when He would have us stretch the boundaries of our friendship to include another.

M*isconception #3: Close friendships involve too much risk.*

When a librarian at our local library learned I was writing a book on friendship, she took a minute to talk. "I've had two close friends in my life," she confided, tears misting her eyes. "Both are dead now. One died of skin cancer. The other died in a car accident. I've just decided never to be close to another person again. It's not worth it. It just hurts too much if you lose them." I could sympathize with her heartache. Losses—especially relational losses—hurt us terribly. Sometimes the loss is caused by a death or unavoidable move. More often, however, friendships are lost over misunderstandings or bitter betrayals. Many emerge from the flames of such conflicts vowing never to be vulnerable again.

But to truly love is to give yourself away. Jesus highlighted the sacrificial nature of Christian friendship when He told His disciples: "Greater love has no one than this, that he lay down his life for his friends" (John 15:13). Then He went on to make His death our example.

Love—true love—is never bought cheaply. As I've interviewed women regarding their friendships, many have shared that those relationships that have grown most deeply have also entailed working through some heartbreaks along the way.

This doesn't mean we share our confidences without discretion. Trust is foundational to any close friendship and earned over the passage of time. If there has been a break in even a small confidence, it may be wise to withhold entrusting more to that person. However, don't let the pain of disappointment keep you from risking friendship again with someone else. C.S. Lewis wrote:

> To love at all is to be vulnerable. Love anything, and your heart will certainly be wrung and possibly be broken. If you want to make sure of keeping it intact . . . lock it up safe in the casket or coffin of your selfishness. But in that casket—safe, dark, motionless, airless—it will change. It will not be broken; it will become unbreakable, impenetrable, unredeemable. (Lewis 1960, 169)

The risks of friendship may indeed seem formidable, but the alternative is even more so.

Misconception #4: "Ministry" is what happens in my involvements at church (teaching Sunday school, singing in the choir, etc.). I don't see my friendships as ministry per se.

The Last Supper was ministry at its best. The events of this evening are without a doubt the most powerful passages in the Gospels. It may be somewhat surprising then to notice the relational context in which Jesus' ministry to His friends took place.

Jesus and His disciples had gathered in the guest room of one of Jesus' followers to eat the Passover meal. As the evening unfolded, Jesus rose from the table, poured water into a basin and knelt next to one disciple after another washing the dust from their road-weary feet. In so doing, He gave them an extraordinary lesson in servanthood they would never forget. Then He took a goblet of wine and a loaf of bread and imbued this simple fare with the significance of His death. It was a powerful night. Jesus taught them as never before. Behind it all was a feeling of intimacy, a sense of urgency and a sigh of sorrow. Jesus said,

> Greater love has no one than this, that he lay down his life for his friends. You are my friends if you do what I command. I no longer call you servants, because a servant does not know his master's business. Instead, I have called you friends, for everything that I learned from my Father I have made known to you. (John 15:13-15)

This group of men—11 simple disciples—were Jesus' friends. Certainly Jesus' ministry had made time for the crowds as well. His teaching and healing abilities were known throughout the region. Hadn't He just entered Jerusalem astride a donkey to the cheers and praises of those lining the streets? Yet Jesus also saw this time around the table with His trusted friends as valid ministry.

I think we have a tendency to so impersonalize ministry that we fail to see what God would accomplish in and through those He's placed in our lives. We tend to see ministry as a specific role we play at church such as singing in the choir, helping in the nursery, teaching Sunday school or having someone new over for dinner. Although such ministry is hardly impersonal, mentally we draw a line between those involvements and having lunch with a friend.

While many friendships grow out of shared ministry experiences, I think we shortchange the Lord when we walk out the church doors thinking our ministry is over until next week. Jesus wants His presence to permeate every aspect of our lives. This doesn't mean that we try to force some deeply spiritual focus on every phone call or lunch date. What it does mean is that we should expect that God will do great things in and through our friendships. It means committing yourself to pray for your friends, seeing God's hand in bringing you together and recognizing His presence in the midst of your sharing. When we view friendship as ministry, time spent with friends becomes more than simple fun. It becomes an eternal investment as well.

The disciples traveled, sacrificed and lived with Jesus for three years. They probably seldom, if ever, thought consciously about the blending of friendship and ministry between themselves and their Lord. Yet in the end, the disciples authored the Gospels telling Jesus' story as only those close to Him could do. The result was that Jesus' friendship with His disciples left a life-giving legacy for the world. Your friendships can touch lives in ways unimaginable when you include them in your definition of ministry.

Misconception #5: Close friendships happen within one's peer group.

I used to think that the best prospects for friendship would be women with children who were near my age and who shared similar values and interests. Thumbing through our first pastorate's directory, I passed over the names of many older women and decided I was doomed to isolation. It was a foolish verdict, grounded in an equally foolish concept. Although shared experiences, interests and values tend to bind people together, differences in age need not be a barrier. In fact, I've discovered that older women often bring a refreshing perspective on life and a wealth of experience that I've often found lacking in peer relationships. Sometimes my friendship and family has filled a void in their lives as well. My experience has been that friendship with older women can be a wonderful, two-way exchange.

Not that my observation is any novel discovery. The Bible describes several friendships spanning generation gaps. Ruth's relationship with her mother-in-law, Naomi, is one such friendship. Through Ruth, Naomi found undying love, provision and family. Through Naomi, Ruth found faith in God and the courage to identify with the Jewish people.

Not only does the Bible give us examples of cross-generational friendships, but it also exhorts older women to train younger women in the art of homemaking. "Then they can train the younger women to love their husbands and children, to be self-controlled and pure, to be busy at home, to be kind, and to be subject to their husbands, so that no one will malign the word of God" (Titus 2:4-5). What better context to do so than through Christian friendship?

The time had come again for us to make another move. The rental truck was parked next to the parsonage loaded a little heavier than it had been when we moved four years earlier. In the gray light of the empty sanctuary, Mary and I embraced and wept openly. It was at church that we had met, so it somehow seemed fitting that it was here that we said our goodbyes.

I can't tell you exactly when our friendship began. Living in the parsonage, our paths crossed frequently in the course of church life. Even though I liked Mary from the start, I didn't expect an older woman could become a close friend. But when the typical struggles of motherhood and the stresses of ministry threatened to break me, Mary seemed like a safe person to confide in. I am glad I did. In time, the sharing went both ways. Over countless cups of tea in her kitchen we shared laughter, wisdom and prayer. Through our friendship I found confidence to mother the children that

God had given me, courage to trust God in new steps of faith and healing from my past.

When the Lord moved us to the Midwest, I thought I'd never survive emotionally. But over the miles and years since Mary and I parted, our bond in the Lord has held true. Today, through her prayers and letters, Mary is still shaping my life with God's love and strengthening me to follow His leading.

The lesson here is simple. Don't let age differences block your path to friendship. God may have some wonderful experiences in store for you through those you'd least expect.

M*isconception #6: I don't have time for friendship.*

It was a cool midsummer day in Seattle and I was doing my first radio interview. The interview allowed listeners to call in and respond to the topic of friendship for ministry wives. A woman who had been a pastor's wife for 10 years called and said:

> I never had a best friend until last year because I was too busy doing all the things I thought I should be doing, being with all the people I thought I should be with. I never knew you could have a close friendship.

Busyness is one of the top plagues of relationships. One person described busyness as the "enemy of friendships." Our crowded schedules steal our time and energy leaving us fatigued and lonely. Yet the stark truth is that we make time for the things that are important to us. So the real question isn't: *Am I too busy for friendship?* Rather, the question is: *Is friendship important enough to take a place of priority in my schedule?* Practically it means uncluttering our schedules to allow for interaction.

Solomon was the wisest and wealthiest king in Israel's history. The Bible says,

> God gave Solomon wisdom and very great insight. . . . Solomon's wisdom was greater than the wisdom of all the men of the East. . . . He was wiser than any other man. (1 Kings 4:29-31)

Fortunately some of that wisdom has been preserved for us. In Proverbs 27 Solomon shares some amazing insights on friendship. He warns,

> Do not forsake your friend and the friend of your father, and do not go to your brother's house when disaster strikes you—better a neighbor nearby than a brother far away. (27:10)

Is friendship important enough to make time for it? The biblical answer is "yes". Even the glorious King Solomon knew life is tough and none of us are strong enough to go the course alone. This is part of the purpose God has in mind for friendship. You may be able to navigate the positive parts of life alone, but you'll wish you had invested more of your heart in friendship when you hit the rough times.

The ministry wife who called in on the radio program not only shared her misconception, but she also shared how God had changed her perspective on friendship. She said: "I've had to give up being everywhere to be with a close friend. Yet it has made all the difference in my life."

Friendship will bless your life, too. Make time for friends.

Misconception #7: My friends really don't need me.

Being the self-centered creatures that we are, most of us seldom stop to think whether our friends need us. We certainly know when loneliness or discouragement stalks our own hearts but knowing the needs of others is not as easy. Philippians 2:4 says, "Each of you should look not only to your own interests, but also to the interests of others." It's a sobering thought. Whether we think we are accountable to our friends or not, God holds us accountable. None of us has the liberty of operating solo.

What does this mean? First, I think it means we stay in touch with our friends enough to know what's happening in their lives. Obviously we have only so much time to go around. God holds us accountable for those He's placed in our lives in a significant way—our spouses, children, relatives and close friends. He may add others to the list from time to time. With regard to friends, we are accountable for those whom we consider "close."

Second, as we become aware of their needs, we should pray and ask God how He might want us to minister to them. He may direct us to make a phone call, drop a card in the mail, share some hand-me-downs or a casserole. Then again, prayer may be our only role for the moment.

Third, we need to encourage friends in their walks with Christ. This includes attending Bible study, church or other activities together on a regular basis. There's nothing quite like walking into a room and seeing that special someone. The moment that your eyes meet, an unspoken spark of welcome warms your heart. You are no longer alone. This is why Hebrews 10:24-25 says:

> Let us consider how we may spur one another on toward love and good deeds. Let us not give up meeting together, as some are in the habit of doing, but let us encourage one another—and all the more as you see the Day approaching.

How can we "spur one another on toward love and good deeds"? Start by showing up regularly at some place of spiritual growth.

Where I live, there are many "good" reasons to neglect church. Recreational opportunities abound and tend to lure even the most de-voted. We are tempted to think, "Hey, I'll pray and do Bible study while I'm fishing or lying on the beach. What difference does it make to God where I worship?" But it does matter. It matters because your absence discourages your friends. It most assuredly discourages your pas-tor. They all need to see your support in a tan-gible way. They need to know that if you didn't show up, there was probably a good reason.

We each have many involvements in life, and we all need cheerleaders to urge us on. One spring I worked as assistant coach for the local junior high school track team. I loved the kids and loved the job. At every track meet I would yell myself hoarse cheering for our team. Some kids placed and some didn't. It was the challenge of seeing each one finish that thrilled my heart. The team thought I was pretty funny screaming and jumping up and down the way I did. Yet behind their ribbing I could tell my enthusiasm meant a lot. I couldn't help but notice that, for too many kids, I was the only one cheering. It's not surprising that later I was able to lead one of those teens to faith in Christ. My involvement had proved my friendship.

Ours is a convenience-minded society. If you don't want to make dinner, just zap some en-tree in the microwave. No time to sit at the ta-ble to eat, you say? There's a fast food restaurant just around the corner. We have disposable everything—from diapers to contact lenses. But close friendships aren't built on convenience, and they aren't disposable. If you want close friendships, you need to get involved and stay involved. There are no shortcuts.

How friendly is your Christianity? Is your life fragrant with the relational fruit of the Holy Spirit or have you settled for something less? (see Galatians 5:22–23). Perhaps you've settled for relationships that are somewhat impersonal, yet comfortably safe. Or perhaps you've immersed yourself in the church to the point that you have no time to really relate. Have you unwittingly made independence your god? This happens in Christian circles more than you might think. Don't let Satan deceive you. Interdependence, not independence, is God's design. In fact, God's place for friendship in ministry is the subject we'll consider in the next chapter.

MAKING IT YOURS

1. What are some misconceptions you've had about friendship?

2. Which of these seven misconceptions tend to reflect your thinking about Christian friendship?

3. If we expand our definition of ministry to include "time spent with friends," what

practical steps will we need to take to allow such ministry to happen?

4. Does James 2:1-9 mean we don't have the right to close friendships as Christians? Explain.

5. What are some steps we can take to apply Philippians 2:4 to the friendships God has given us?

6. How has friendship with an older person blessed your life? How might such a friendship be a blessing? (see Titus 2:3-5)

7. What can you do to encourage your friendships to be Christ-centered, not self-centered?

Chapter 2

Killing the Lone Ranger

He thundered onto my television screen astride his white stallion. As his horse reared magnificently, he would call out with upraised hand, "High Ho, Silver. Away!" Through the magic of television I would follow the Lone Ranger into another stirring episode of western bravado. His solitary style of leadership was an echo from the past; the style of leadership we are envision for ourselves and our church leaders today. But it is not a leadership style supported by Scripture.

Jonah's Example

In contrast, Scripture presents several disparaging biographies of solo ministry. One of these was Jonah. Perhaps one of the reasons that Jonah chose to minister alone was that he really didn't want to minister at all! When God told him to go and preach to the people of Nineveh, Jonah ran as far as he could in the opposite direction.

Few of us look for travel companions when we are on the run from responsibility. Friends have that uncomfortable way of asking questions and raising doubts when we fly in the face of good judgment. They say things like:

"Do you really think marriage will be that much better with someone else?"
"What about your family? What about your commitment to the Lord?"
"I don't think I could do that."

I wonder if Jonah would have traveled as far as he did if he'd taken a friend along. Somehow, I rather doubt it.

Running alone, Jonah made quick progress. He soon found himself in Joppa where he was able to buy passage on a ship bound for Tarshish. In Jonah's day, Tarshish was the outer edge of the civilized world. It's no wonder Jonah felt he would be too far away for God to see.

After leaving port, however, the ship was caught in a violent storm. The sailors jettisoned the cargo to lighten the ship. It was not enough. In desperation they dragged Jonah out of the hold and begged for him to pray to his God. Jonah had told them that he was on the run from God. But these men had heard of many gods. They paid little heed as to why this Jew wanted passage to Tarshish. Yet as the situation became more intense, the sailors began to question Jonah.

"He answered, 'I am a Hebrew and I worship the LORD, the God of heaven, who made the sea and the land' " (Jonah 1:9). Suddenly the sailors realized that this storm might be retribution by Jonah's God.

Terrified, they asked, "What should we do to you to make the sea calm down for us?"

"Pick me up and throw me into the sea," replied Jonah (1:11-12). The sailors resisted. Instead they tried again to reach land, but the storm only continued to escalate. Finally there was no other choice. They prayed:

> "O LORD, please do not let us die for taking this man's life. Do not hold us accountable for killing an innocent man, for you, O LORD, have done as you pleased." Then they took Jonah and threw him overboard. . . . (1:14-15)

Sinking beneath the waves, Jonah instantly became fish food. When he came to his senses later, he realized he was in the stomach of a huge fish. Alone in the damp and the dark, Jonah repented of his rebellion. He would go to Nineveh and preach if that's what God wanted him to do. Besides God's forgiveness, Jonah also received free passage to Assyria, where the fish vomited him up on the beach. Not the best start for a ministry perhaps, but a beginning all the same.

Several days later Jonah arrived in Nineveh, but his heart was as bitter as ever. He didn't like the Ninevites and he was angry that God would have compassion on an enemy of Israel.

It's no wonder Jonah didn't like the Ninevites. Known for their military might, they would emerge into periods of incredible power and then slide into political remission. During their "active" phases they exercised brutal military tactics intending to intimidate their enemies into submission.

Yet as Jonah preached, the people repented. From the king to the lowliest child, the residents of Nineveh fasted and clothed themselves in sackcloth. God heard their prayers and withheld His judgment.

Some might have viewed this as one of the greatest revivals of ancient times, but not Jonah.

> O LORD, is this not what I said when I was still at home? That is why I was so quick to flee to Tarshish. I knew that you are a gracious and compassionate God, slow to anger and abounding in love, a God who relents from sending calamity. Now, O LORD, take away my life, for it is better for me to die than to live. (4:2-3)

Jonah was suicidally depressed. God reasoned with Jonah's heart, but no further mention is ever made of this wayward prophet. God's judgment on Nineveh was temporarily averted, but whether Jonah continued in ministry is unknown.

We all need friends to keep us on track when we are tempted to wander. Look closely at the lives of those that have strayed from God's will and you'll discover a lack of godly friendship. Too often isolation becomes the breeding ground for temptation and sin.

Such was the case with Tim. Tim and his wife, Linda, had been married for eight years. They did things together and talked often. Neither of them considered their marriage to be headed for trouble. Yet selfish interests insidiously wedged their way into their hearts over time, stealing their joy and undermining their commitment to one another. When Tim became the object of another woman's attention, he was ripe for temptation. Before he realized it, Tim was soon drawn into a flirtation that threatened to end his marriage. With God's help, Tim and Linda's marriage survived, but only after a painful period of rebuilding.

Tim and Linda's story is all too common today. We look at it and see the obvious symptoms: selfishness, lack of commitment, etc. But the break in their relationship happened during a time when they were really very lonely. One day as we visited over coffee I asked them about this period in their lives. "Did you have some friends that you were able to talk to about this whole situation?" I asked.

"No," Tim responded. "As far as friendships in our lives at that time, we just didn't have any friends. If we had lived near my best friend, and I had told him of this situation, he would have straightened me out right away. But no, there was no one like that in my life at that time." Tim's experience echoes the lesson of Jonah's life—isolation breeds vulnerability.

Instead God intends that godly friendship would help us keep watch over one another's hearts. This is why James 5:19-20 says:

> My brothers, if one of you should wander from the truth and someone should bring him back, remember this: Whoever turns a sinner from the error of his way will save him from death and cover over a multitude of sins.

Godly friends are the guardrails on our road through life. Without them, Satan can easily distract and lure us into driving off a precipice along life's way.

God also intends Christian friendship to not only confront one another in obvious areas of sin, but also to challenge one another to godly living in smaller ways as well.

I love mysteries. In my thinking, there's nothing better than an unhurried rainy day and a spellbinding mystery. Today I seldom have the time for such an indulgence, but there was a time when I read mysteries avidly. One of my favorite writers, however, had the practice of including sensual scenes and dialogue along with the story line. The material bothered my conscience, but I simply rationalized my way around it and read on.

Then one day as I was talking about one such mystery with a friend she made a simple comment that shook my complacency. "You know," she said half joking, half seriously, "you shouldn't be reading that stuff." Those words went right to my heart. I knew it was true. Our lives are affected by what fills our minds. The sensual parts of my favorite mysteries had no place in my thoughts as a Christian. I've since sworn off that author's books and become very selective about my fictional reading. It didn't seem a big thing at the time, but I know that practice dulled the fervency of my walk with Christ. How thankful I am for a friend who challenged my temptation to compromise.

"As iron sharpens iron, so one man sharpens another" says Proverbs 27:17. We all need those who will dare to confront and challenge us. Perhaps the book of Jonah would read much differently had he taken time for such friendships in his own life.

Elijah's Example

Elijah was another prophet who ministered alone. Unlike Jonah, Elijah ministered in harmony with God's will. And what a powerful ministry he had. As a result of the miraculous contest atop Mount Carmel, Israel repented of its idolatry and killed hundreds of the prophets of Baal (See 1 Kings 18:40). Yet following Elijah's revival service atop Mount Carmel, he experienced a crushing blow that almost ended his ministry completely.

Queen Jezebel, the chief promoter of Baal worship in Israel, was furious when she heard what had happened. She promptly put out a contract on Elijah's life. In terror, Elijah ran into the desert alone. In the next verse he prayed, "I have had enough, LORD . . . Take my life" (19:4).

There most certainly were many factors involved in the onset of Elijah's depression. Physical and emotional exhaustion, stress, hunger being some of these factors. In time the depression passed and Elijah again welcomed God's call to ministry. Of the three commissions given him, the last was to anoint Elisha as his successor (19:16). It was the first commission Elijah hurried to fulfill. You see, Elijah had learned an important lesson in the desert: There is safety in numbers. Only a fool leads alone.

Rick Moen is one of the most talented youth ministers I've ever met. Under his leadership, the youth programs at the three churches where he has ministered have all grown and done phenomenal things. Yet, I was surprised to find that a busy youth pastor like Rick was also a man deeply committed to friendship.

In a taped interview Rick related the following.

In my schooling, I remember the president of the college saying "If you are going to be a pastor, you are going to choose not to have friends" I thought at the time that something was wrong with that, but he couched it in a spiritual setting of sacrifice. Certainly solo leadership was the leadership style modeled for me by my pastor, and the pastor at the first church where I was employed. But within three years I began to realize that I just wasn't doing well leading alone. Rather than leave the ministry, I began to develop a youth staff.

"It began essentially as an extension of the youth ministry. By that, I mean that I worked with them on ministry related issues. Then I began to realize that these relationships needed to extend to my life outside of work as well. I couldn't, in good conscience, say, 'Lead with me in my work, but you have no business in my life, my parenting, my marriage or major financial decisions.' This realization eventually led to establishing a covenant relationship with several closer friends.

"I can't begin to express how profoundly those friendships have impacted my life! I probably would not be where I am today, professionally or spiritually, if not for the impact of those relationships. It was a relationship that worked both ways. I know for a fact, that one of my friends would be divorced today if not for the challenge of my friendship in his life during that critical time."

It has been said that we all need both a Nathan and a Jonathan in our lives. We need a "Nathan" (the prophet who boldly confronted David with his sin) to get us back on course when we go astray. We need a "Jonathan" (David's faithful friend) who will love us no matter what. Fortunate is the one who finds both qualities in one person. Without one or the other, life's pitfalls pose extra dangers.

Christ's Example

Christ, on the other hand, was continually accompanied by his disciples. For three years this band of 12 men lived together as a family. They argued with one another. They challenged one another. They shared the hardships of the road and they grew to love one another.

Discipleship was the obvious product of such exposure, but there was more here than a discipleship program. Christ needed the disciples, just as they needed Him. Jesus had been called to a difficult ministry of confrontation. As the crowds criticized and forsook Him, Jesus turned to His disciples.

"You do not want to leave too, do you?" Jesus asked the Twelve.

Simon Peter answered him, "Lord, to whom shall we go? You have the words of eternal life. We believe and know that you are the Holy One of God." (John 6:67-69)

How Peter's words must have encouraged Jesus. It is not surprising that Peter became one of Jesus' three closest friends. In the Garden of Gethsemane, Jesus would call His three friends—Peter, James and John—apart to pray with Him. In their presence Jesus let down all barriers, inviting them to share His grief.

"My soul is overwhelmed with sorrow to the point of death," He said. "Stay here and keep watch with me" (Matthew 26:38). Later when He hung on a rough Roman cross, Jesus confidently entrusted His mother to John's care (see John 19:26-27). Even as the Son of God, Jesus knew the importance of Christian friendship with regard to His ministry.

The Apostle's Example

Unlike the Lone Ranger style of leadership, tandem leadership was also seen in the ministry of the apostles. As the Church began to grow it would have been tempting to try and cover more territory by sending the apostles out as solo missionaries. Certainly there must have been some that went alone. Phillip is one such example. The norm for leadership, however, seems to have been a team effort. So we read in Acts 3 and 4 of the joint ministry of Peter and John. Later in Acts 11 we read of Barnabas' friendship with the unlikely missionary, Paul.

We seldom recognize this, but much of Paul's ministry happened because of his friendship with Barnabas. It was Barnabas who first believed Paul's conversion. The Christians in Jerusalem were skeptical and afraid of Paul. After all, he was known far and wide as a persecutor of the Church. Barnabas alone took Paul's word and gained him acceptance into Christian circles. Later, as Barnabas watched the spread of Christianity to the Gentiles, he brought Paul to Antioch to minister with him among the Christian community there. For a year, the two men did the basics of church planting. When the year ended, the Antioch Christians ordained Paul and Barnabas to do a similar missionary effort in the world at large. Thus began the spread of Christianity and Paul's famous missionary journeys. None of this would have been possible, however, if not for the faith and persistence of Barnabas.

The team of Paul and Barnabas later was replaced by two teams: Barnabas and John Mark in Cyprus, and Paul and Silas in Syria and beyond. Teamwork was a trademark of Paul's leadership from the beginning until his death in Rome. Several of his letters were written to friends (Timothy, Titus and Philemon). As he faced his final days in a Roman prison, he wrote to Timothy:

Do your best to come to me quickly, for

Demas, because he loved this world, has deserted me and has gone to Thessalonica. Crescens has gone to Galatia, and Titus to Dalmatia. Only Luke is with me. Get Mark and bring him with you, because he is helpful to me in my ministry. (2 Timothy 4:9-11)

Was Paul some kind of wimp? Hardly. Wimps don't keep going after being beaten, jailed, shipwrecked or suffering any of the other hardships Paul endured. Instead, Paul was a godly missionary with a clear understanding of the merit of team ministry.

Considering these biblical examples, could it be that a disservice is done not only to those we lead, but also to ourselves as we plod doggedly along in our Lone Ranger approach to ministry? The biblical answer is "yes". Still, individual leadership seems to be the rule rather than the exception wherever you look—including within the church.

I asked Rick Moen why this tends to be true. "American culture has individualism as its god," Rick responded. "It's individualism everywhere you go—especially male individualism. It is a creed in our culture that you are to go it alone. I call it the Myth of Independence. Unfortunately the Church is more like the world than it even realizes. Yet worldly principles can only yield worldly results. One of those false principles, I believe, is individual leadership."

Four Reasons for Team Leadership

Solomon was the wisest king that ever sat on the Hebrew throne. He was also a prolific writer. Among his writings are these words on friendship:

> Two are better than one,
>   because they have a good return for
>   their work:
> If one falls down,
>   his friend can help him up.
> But pity the man who falls
>   and has no one to help him up!
> Also, if two lie down together, they will
>   keep warm.
>   But how can one keep warm alone?
> Though one may be overpowered,
>   two can defend themselves.
> A cord of three strands is not quickly
>   broken.
>   (Ecclesiastes 4:9-12)

Solomon made several points about the merit of friendship. First, teamwork is more productive. Remember the old adage: "If you want it done right, you have to do it yourself!" The verses from Ecclesiastes contradict such reasoning. Certainly we all need to choose our companions wisely. You don't invite a two-year-old to help you weed your flower bed. But common sense also suggests that two pairs of hands in a weedy garden pull far more weeds than one pair toiling alone. The same is true whatever your ministry. Add a teammate and the return on your joint labor will be greatly increased.

Second, there is protection in friendship. My friend, Pam, tells the story of a summit attempt she and her husband once made on Mount Rainier. It was early morning. Pam and Dave were roped up with two others to work their way across a glacier en route to the summit. A deep crevasse barred their way. Fortunately drifting snow had compacted into a fragile bridge spanning the gap. Tentatively three of them crossed the snow bridge without incident. Then as Dave stepped onto the bridge it disintegrated, plummeting him into the yawning crevasse below. On the glacier above his wife and two friends instinctively dug into the ice breaking his fall. Later they lowered equipment to Dave, enabling him to climb out of the crevasse. Without their assistance Dave would have fallen to certain injury, perhaps even death. Instead, because of the rope between them, tragedy was averted.

Life is full of pitfalls. Both Elijah and Jonah discovered that leading solo is also leaving yourself wide open to disaster if your footing fails. Godly friendship, on the other hand, provides a safety net. It renews perspective when you lean toward arrogance or despair. When you live in isolation, it's all too easy to hear only the tempter's voice. As Solomon says, "Pity the man who falls and has no one to help him up!"

Third, there is warm fellowship in friendship. Any wilderness survival course eventually talks about hypothermia. Hypothermia is when a person's body temperature falls below normal; through exposure the person is chilled beyond his capacity to warm himself. Left unaided, an exposed person's body temperature will continue to drop until he dies.

Hypothermia is combated in several ways. If your friend is chilled, bundle him up in extra clothes or a blanket. If your friend is still cold, the next step is to get him up and moving, and make him drink something hot. In extreme cases where the person is too cold to cooperate with these efforts, it is recommended that you put two people together in a sleeping bag. This way the body heat of the one will warm the other.

This is the idea reflected in Ecclesiastes 4:11. Left alone, a person can easily freeze to death. Only the coziness of shared warmth can cut a deadly chill—whether physical or spiritual.

It has been said that the deepest friendships have been forged in foxholes. Watch a group of reunited veterans and you'll see honest, unabashed, loving friendships. Many refer to those they knew in combat as their closest friends. Ironic though it may be, going through experiences together brings a warmth to life.

Solitude, on the other hand, is not only scary, but downright uncomfortable.

Fourth, Solomon reminds us that we are more effective in spiritual warfare if we adopt a tandem leadership style. Animals who travel in packs and herds know this survival principle instinctively. When threatened, elephants form a tight unit with their formidable tusks and trunks facing the enemy. In this manner, no predator can approach unnoticed. Indeed, most predators know that the best target is the one most easily culled from the rest.

Satan knows this as well. Alone, we've no one to watch our flanks. Together we are a formidable team. When we include Christ in our friendships, we are unbeatable.

Have you been trying to minister as a Lone Ranger Christian—just you and God against the world? I have good news for you. Solo ministry is not God's design. It's time to kill the Lone Ranger image. After all, even the Lone Ranger had Tonto, a faithful friend who rode beside him.

MAKING IT YOURS

1. Be honest with yourself. Whose style of ministry do you most closely emulate—Elijah or Paul?

2. What are the strengths of tandem leadership? (Ecclesiastes 4:9-12)

3. What are the weaknesses of solo leader-ship?

4. Do you agree with Rick Moen's comments on leadership in American culture? Explain.

5. Proverbs 27:17 says, "As iron sharpens iron, so one man sharpens another." How has God used friends to challenge you in your walk with God?

6. Read one or all of the Last Supper accounts in the Gospels (Matthew 26:20-35; Mark 14:12-31; Luke 22:14-38; John 13-17). What would tandem leadership look like in your own ministry?

7. The ministry of Paul might never have hap-pened if not for Barnabas. Is there someone you need to befriend and disciple?

Chapter 3

Loneliness: Learning to Live with Transition

I dialed Mary's telephone number for the third time in a week. I don't know what magic I thought would happen over the 2,000 plus miles of phone lines separating us. All I knew was that I was achingly lonely. It felt so good to hear her familiar voice.

Americans are a people on the move. While the percentage of Americans relocating is dropping, statistics show that 45.1 million Americans still move every year. True, most of those moves are from house to house within the same county (61percent). But the remaining 39 percent make moves outside that area—moves entailing changes in a family's entire social network (DeAre 1993, 10-11).

No one feels this transition deeper than the wife. When our family moved from the Pacific Northwest to Omaha, Nebraska, I was faced with an immense adjustment. I found myself often unconsciously searching for the familiar landmarks I'd left behind. "Is this the street I take to the school, or do I turn at the next one?" I wondered hesitantly. Even the simplest outings became real challenges.

Yet my biggest adjustments following a move are the social ones. I don't like feeling lonely. It's a yucky, gray, empty feeling. One author described it as "a feeling of discontent and rejection . . . a sense of being helpless, trapped in a physical or emotional limbo" (Schultz 1976, 15). Generally, loneliness is a subject we avoid thinking about, a topic rarely mentioned and a feeling that is often repressed. However it's described, loneliness is uncomfortable at best and crippling at its worst. And although I never pack it in a box, I've found loneliness moves with me wherever I go. I think there are three reasons for this.

1. Separation from Loved Ones

In the Victorian classic, *Anne of Avonlea*, the author captures the pain of moving as Anne bids farewell to her elderly friend, Miss Lavender. "Yes, I'm going," said Anne. "I'm very glad with my head . . . and very sorry with my heart" (Montgomery 1909, 271). It's an experience all of us who have moved can relate to. The cognitive part of us knows the necessity of moving and is glad, while at the same time the emotional side of us grieves.

I left my dearest friend when we moved to our first pastorate, a small congregation in western Washington. Cheryl and I had shared so much during our two years of friendship. We had our first babies about the same time, attended the same church, went to the same Bible study and even lived in the same apartment building the last two months before our move to Washington. I knew moving away would hurt. I just didn't know how much.

Several months after we'd moved, Cheryl came to visit. We spent a wonderful week together, laughing and talking just like old times. But the day I took her to the train station and said goodbye my world fell apart. I'll never know how I negotiated the freeway traffic home, for I was in tears the whole way. Cheryl was returning to the familiar world I'd left behind, and I to the unfamiliar. What's more, I was neither sure how strong our friendship would remain over the miles, nor could I imagine anything growing in my heart to fill her empty space.

Dee Brestin, in her book, *Friendships of Women*, shares her pain when God has moved her on. She writes, "Separating me from the women friends who have nourished me and strengthened me . . . is a severe trauma. I feel as if I am starving, and I pray God will connect me with new women friends before I wither and die" (Brestin 1988, 16). It's true—women are relational creatures, and as such we have deep emotional needs. When moving cuts the ties to those we love, we grieve. This is one reason why the first year after a move can be so lonely. Friendships take time to develop, and I haven't found any shortcuts. So with every move, I find I'm occasionally lonely.

2. Unrealistic Expectations

Another reason we often experience intense loneliness that first year is because reality usually falls short of our expectations. I imagined our first pastorate would be a sunshine experience. My home would always be filled with congenial, smiling people that I would be delighted to entertain. Our little church would grow as it had never done before. Somewhere along the way we would unknowingly slip into a cozy niche in a community that welcomed us with open arms. It was a wonderful dream, but I couldn't have been more wrong.

Through the first two years we discovered that things were radically different from our rosy expectations. People came burdened with problems, not the desire to socialize. Our cozy little community was plagued with drug, alcohol and family abuse. We didn't exactly fit the expectations of our congregation either. After a year together, neither side seemed convinced that we liked each other. Any romantic dreams of ministry in the country I had once entertained were now replaced with my desperate desire to return to the city life I once knew.

It wasn't that our previous life in Portland, Oregon, was so grand. I experienced disillusionment when we first moved there too. When my husband and I first talked of moving to Western Evangelical Seminary for Scott's schooling, I welcomed the thought of entering a close knit academic community. I didn't foresee the nights we'd hear the upstairs neighbor, Brian, snoring away, or our next door neighbor slamming his front door and causing our pictures to slide in disarray countless times.

In time we developed treasured memories in both Portland and western Washington, but at each place I needed to adjust my expectations. No matter where I've moved or how green the grass appeared on the other side, no place was exactly what it seemed to be. This type of disappointment added to the loneliness of that initial year.

3. *Cultural Clashes*

A third reason loneliness haunts the first year in a new place is due to the cultural adjustments. I moved to rural America from an urban background, having grown up in the context of crowded schools and large churches. My family had always been pretty independent from relatives. Instead, our social life centered on our friends from church.

Then I entered a community that was almost totally interdependent. Indeed, it took several years for me to figure out who belonged to whom and how. People in the town grew up, married and settled there. It was a way of life incomprehensible to a family with shallow roots like ours. Since everyone related socially within their extended family structures, we often felt left out. I can't count the weekends we invited someone to join us for an activity only to find that they were busy with relatives. We had no relatives there and ended up being an island unto ourselves. It was frustrating and desperately lonely. Holidays were especially tough. How grateful I was for friends who had the graciousness to include us in their plans at such times.

Gone were my usual social outlets. No malls. No theaters. No restaurants. Life was rougher—tougher—here in this logging town at the foot of the mountains. For me, everything needed to be rediscovered and redefined.

As I became better acquainted with small town life, I began to ask: "What's wrong with me? Why don't I fit in? Do I want to fit in?" These were deep questions, indicating my culturally based search for identity. Then one day I met Gwen on my way to the market for milk. Her weary looking farm truck, loaded with split wood, was parked outside the local garage awaiting its hundredth repair. As Gwen stepped from beside the truck to say hello, I noticed her arm was in a sling.

"What happened to you?" I asked earnestly.

"Oh, that," she answered nonchalantly. "I was cutting a tree down and it fell on me and broke my arm."

"A tree fell on you?" I responded in near amazement.

"Yeah, this is nothing. You should see the burn I got from the chain saw muffler!"

I didn't stay to see the nasty muffler burn, but later commented to my husband, "If you *ever* see me wielding a chain saw, pack and get me out of here! We will have been here too long." Experiences like that taught me the difference in the definition of a woman's role in the town. Neither side was wrong. In fact, I rather admired Gwen's hardy pioneer spirit. Still, I had different goals for myself, and learning to wield a chain saw just wasn't one of them.

Any major move in distance or social environment brings cultural differences. Even changing churches can present an entirely new approach to worship. Again, it is usually not a matter of right or wrong. Such changes require adjustments which may mean a new way of looking at a situation or a new way of doing something. The more quickly we can adapt without feeling that we've compromised the things we want to hold on to, the less loneliness we'll experience. As long as we struggle with adapting to what's new but necessary, a sense of isolation can prevail.

The loneliness characteristic of transition

usually lasts from a year to 18 months. During that time, most people are able to connect with some new friends and adjust to their surroundings. But the feeling of belonging can seem like a long time in coming. Fortunately, God offers some perspectives that can help take the sting out of transitional loneliness.

Don't Close Your Heart to New Beginnings

God didn't call Naomi and Elimelech to move from Judah to Moab. They made that impetuous decision on their own. In the 10 years that followed, tragedy struck as Naomi lost first her husband then both her sons. Now, totally alone except for her two daughters-in-law, Naomi decided to return to her homeland. Both her daughters-in-law begged to go with her. Naomi insisted they stay in Moab. Orpah finally conceded, but Ruth would not.

> Don't urge me to leave you or to turn back from you. Where you go I will go, and where you stay I will stay. Your people will be my people and your God my God. Where you die I will die, and there I will be buried. May the LORD deal with me, be it ever so severely, if anything but death separates you and me. (Ruth 1:16-17)

What a beautiful pledge of love and loyalty! However, we get no indication that it stirred the heavy heart of Naomi. Instead, when

Naomi saw Ruth's determination, she simply quit urging her to return to Moab. In her loneliness, Naomi gave no response to Ruth's declaration of love and friendship.

So the two women journeyed on together side by side upon the road. Together in a physical sense, but far apart in spirit. Upon reaching Bethlehem, Naomi told her friends, "I went away full, but the LORD has brought me back empty" (Ruth 1:21). Ouch! How Ruth's heart must have ached as she felt the blow of Naomi's rejection. Hadn't God graciously given Naomi a companion in Ruth? She had sacrificed so much to fill that space. Ruth had traded life, perhaps marriage, among her people for an uncertain future in a foreign land with a widowed mother-in-law. Ruth's sacrifices must have seemed little appreciated at that point.

Yet too often I have responded like Naomi. Holding onto the shreds of friendships I've had to leave behind, I've often overlooked the new companions God desires to give me.

It's not that we need to cut ourselves off from old friends. It may take extra planning and effort, but friendships held close over the years—over the miles—are a rich treasure. I'm a big advocate of using the phone, writing to stay in touch and planning visits whenever possible. Life is just too short and friends are too precious to be discarded like dusty bric-a-brac.

But we also err when we cuddle up to loneliness and close our hearts to new beginnings.

Recently I returned to the town in which we first pastored. As I drove toward a friend's home, an elderly neighbor came to mind. *Betty will be hurt if I don't stop*, I thought to myself. So, more out of obligation than desire, I took the time and visited.

We embraced as I prepared to leave. Tears filled her eyes and she spoke brokenly, "I sure love you guys. You know, I pray for you every day." In that moment I grieved. I regretted my hardened heart that had resisted the love she had offered over so many years. God had desired to bless my life through this woman, but I had held her off. We had seemed too different to be friends. Now it was almost too late. In that moment, I realized how much we had both lost and I wept, too.

I've found that it usually takes a year to form several significant friendships. And although I know of no shortcuts, I've found it helps to accept the loneliness of that year as simply part of the move. Then I look expectantly to God to fill my friendship list with the people He's chosen. Some of these become lifetime friendships, other relationships blossom for a season, then fade with time. Yet even in the loneliest places, God has faithfully provided a "Ruth" to walk beside me. She may not have been the companion I expected, but she has indeed been the one He's lovingly chosen.

Parable of an Arrowhead

But what about those friendships we leave behind? How much energy should go into maintaining those relationships? Are there any cautions we should take? These are questions facing anyone making a major move. Certainly the awful tension of having your heart divided is one of the heartaches of transitional loneliness.

One spring our family moved from the West Coast to Omaha, Nebraska. My husband, Scott, interned for a year under the Outreach Pastor at Christ Community Church, thereby specializing in outreach ministry. Following the year of internship, our job search began anew. Only God knew where that search would take us.

While I was excited about the opportunity for Scott to specialize in outreach ministry, my heart ached over the friendships I left behind. One particularly special relationship was my friendship with Mary. As I gazed from our third-story apartment out over the rooftops of Omaha, I agonized over whether I should quit nurturing my friendship with Mary. It hurt to have my heart invested in two places. Perhaps it was hurting her as well. Perhaps it was just better to let things fade and move on. Besides, I had no guarantee I'd ever move back to the Pacific Northwest. It seemed just as likely that we'd move even farther away.

One day as I was praying about this, God mentally took me back to a scene from my childhood. When I was a kid my parents owned a trailer at a lake resort. Every summer my family would move from our home in the city to the resort. There my brothers and I joined the other resort kids in all sorts of adventures. Swimming filled much of our time. We'd dive into the brisk clear water, splash, swim and snorkel until we shivered like autumn leaves before a winter gale. Then leaving our soggy footprints fading on the dock, we'd run for the beach, throwing ourselves down on the coarse, warm pebbles to dry.

Many, many years ago, the Indians had used this spot to gather around a campfire and methodically chip an armament of flint arrowheads. The resort owner had found many arrowheads over the years. I had been in his home once and feasted my eyes enviously on his impressive collection. So as we toasted in the summer sunshine, our hands were always busy sifting through the pebbles and sand, hoping someday we'd find an arrowhead to claim as our own. Finally, one day my persistence was rewarded, and I held in my palm my own precious arrowhead. That was a special find! The arrowhead went into a box in my dresser that has since come to gather other assorted precious bits.

That day in Omaha, as I thought about throwing away my friendship with Mary, God reminded me of that arrowhead. "You know," He seemed to whisper, "the day you found that arrowhead was a golden day, and you've kept that treasure all these years. Wherever you've moved that arrowhead has moved with you. Cheryl, there are many people on the beach of life. Yet only a few become truly precious, and it takes a lot of searching to find them. Mary is such a friend—a gift I've given you. Would you cast away her friendship, while you are willing to prize a simple stone?"

Friendships are special treasures. One author wrote, "All in all, my friendships are the bedrock of my life, the deep current that carries me past obstacles and depression. . . . I hold friends in my heart like a precious jewel in my hand" (Schultz 1976, 101). As Christians, friendships are one form of God's grace to us in human form. True, you can't stay close with all your friends when you move. But there are always a few friends that are special. I've found it's worth the extra effort to continue investing in these relationships. Kindred spirits don't come along every day. Only fools discard what money can't buy and what time may never replace.

A Word of Caution

When God moves us on, we should heed one relational caution regarding the church. If the move is precipitated by an offense or disillusionment within the church, slandering the offending pastor or congregation is wrong especially to those still attending. Slander usually means telling a damaging falsehood about someone, but slander also means telling information that will intentionally hurt another's reputation. Both are wrong. As Christians, we are to "bear with each other and forgive whatever grievances you may have against one another. Forgive as the Lord forgave you" (Colossians 3:13).

Forgiveness can be very hard to do following deep hurts by a pastor or congregation. Not only do we instinctively want to defend our decision to move, but we also feel a sense of duty to warn others about the possible hurts they, too, could experience from Pastor X or the Down-the-Street Community Church. While both motivations are understandable, we need to be very careful that we say nothing to undermine the pastor or ministry that is still taking place.

First Timothy 5:19 says an accusation against a pastor should only be heard when accompanied by similar testimony from several others. Even then the goal is that the pastor might better adjust to the needs of his church. The context of this passage refers to working through difficulties within the local church. It does not apply to external critics. In fact, God warns:

> Whoever slanders his neighbor in secret,
>   him will I put to silence;
> whoever has haughty eyes and a proud
>   heart,
>   him I will not endure. (Psalm 101:5)

Only in regard to heresy or personal endangerment should others be warned. Has the congregation drifted away from Christ and become a cult? Has the pastor added to, or taken away from, the gospel of Christ to such an extent as to change its message? Is he involved in a life of sin that will endanger others? More often, people change churches over petty things instead of doctrinal or moral issues. Yet a change for doctrinal reasons is still a good reason to keep watch over your conversation. For although we have the right to share our own doctrinal convictions, we do not have the right to share the dirty linen of a former congregation. God will avenge the wrong. Justice is His place, not ours.

Embrace Reality

Transitional loneliness can also be eased by digging in and accepting reality. Jeremiah was a God-ordained prophet. In Jeremiah 1:5 God said to him, "Before I formed you in the womb I knew you, before you were born I set you apart; I appointed you as a prophet to the nations."

But by Chapter 20 it is evident that Jeremiah's ministry experience wasn't turning out as he'd expected.

O LORD, you deceived me, . . .
    I am ridiculed all day long;
everyone mocks me. . . .
So the word of the LORD has brought me

insult and reproach all day long.
(20:7-8)

Clearly this was not the reception Jeremiah had envisioned. Even his friends had turned against him.

Life is never what it seems, is it? We often enter a new move with high ambitions and hopes that are usually never realized. Often, like Jeremiah, we end up disappointed and lonely. What's the solution? We need to recognize our romantic ideals for what they are, reject them, dig in and accept reality.

What is reality, you ask? Galatians 6:9 admonishes, "Let us not become weary in doing good, for at the proper time we will reap a harvest if we do not give up." Reality is this: Living God's way—anywhere—is hard work. Satan never surrenders territory easily. Whether the area of disillusionment is at work or at home, living in faithful obedience to God is more often a spiritual battle than a rose garden of delights. The war rages on everywhere; only the battle lines change. Spiritual warfare is intrinsic to Christian living. The payoff is that God honors faithfulness. If we continue to obey Him, He will produce fruit from our efforts.

Every ministry position my husband has held has seemed tiresome and disappointing at times. But loneliness slips away when I relinquish my expectations and focus on the Lord who has called us to serve. Jeremiah discovered the same. In Jeremiah 20:12-13 he comforts himself with these words:

> O Lord Almighty, you who examine the righteous
> and probe the heart and mind, . . .
> to you I have committed my cause.

> Sing to the Lord!
> Give praise to the Lord!
> He rescues the life of the needy
> from the hands of the wicked.

Jeremiah still had some days of deep discouragement. You will, too, but hope always springs eternal in Christ's presence.

Be Creative; Be Flexible

Differences in culture can really bother us if we insist on polarizing them as right or wrong. The truth is that lifestyles differ everywhere. I've found that the more creative and flexible I am, the faster I adjust. Our first pastorate was in a rural community that offered few of the social outlets we were used to. Instead of going to restaurants, shopping malls or theaters, we learned to enjoy short hikes in the surrounding mountains, to swim in the river and to watch football on TV with friends. I developed hobbies and volunteered to help coach the junior high school track team. In many ways, it wasn't a particularly nice place to live, but I found things I could appreciate if I looked for them.

Images—like my daily walk to the post office to visit as I collected my mail, the country western station blaring out over the milk and eggs in the market or even the gray wisps of wood smoke curling up into the morning mist when the weary, comfortable town still seemed half asleep—these, and countless others, are memories I resisted at first, yet eventually I learned to cherish them. I have learned that there's something to enjoy wherever you go. Just make up your mind to look for it.

What Can Be Learned?

A final perspective that has helped me through transitional loneliness from a move has been to ask God how I can use such a period in my life. As I interviewed people about their friendships, I inevitably asked whether they had experienced a time of intense loneliness. Then I asked if there seemed a God-given purpose in that experience. The answer has always been affirmative for both questions. One woman said, "God wanted me to learn to depend more on Him." Another person said, "God showed me I had a lot to learn about developing relationships." Others offered different reasons. Personally, the loneliness from one move gave me the time to write my first book. The relational emptiness in my life at that time provided space for creativity in other areas.

In contrast to what we often feel, loneliness need not be a negative experience. It is in the quiet of those times that God can often minister in a unique way. Craig Ellison, in his book *Loneliness "The Search for Intimacy,"* wrote:

> Another fringe benefit of loneliness is that it provides us with a chance to learn positive solitude. . . . It's using the time and silence to get in touch with ourselves, with God, and with our future. (Ellison 1980, 151)

And renowned speaker and author, Jill Briscoe, testifies:

> Loneliness is still an unwelcome guest, but looking back I know it affords me space to develop friendships and ministry skills I would never develop any other way. (Briscoe 1991, 121)

God has a purpose in the empty spaces He allows in our lives. Perhaps we ought to embrace loneliness rather than run from it. Are you lonely? If so, ask God how He wants to use the empty spaces in your heart. You might be surprised at His answer. Even the emptiness may be part of His plan for you.

God has moved my family many times. Many of our moves have meant relocating out of state. As we unpacked last time, we said, half-jokingly (my husband was joking, I wasn't) that this was our final move. I certainly hope so. I'm tired of goodbyes and hellos. To be honest, I'm tired of awkward, lonely, first year transitions. Yet wherever God leads, I know He is sufficient. For although loneliness moves with me, God's presence is there as well. I'm never really alone. I can always see Him through the eyes of faith, if I'll just adjust my perspective.

Making It Yours

1. Have you ever moved? What was the hardest adjustment you faced?

2. Even though Naomi initially closed her heart to Ruth's love, Ruth persisted. What testimony do the women of Bethlehem give regarding the merit of Ruth's friendship in Ruth 4:15? How should this challenge us to embrace new relationships that God brings into our lives following a move?

3. How can staying in touch with those you've left behind bring encouragement even as you face adjustments in a new place? (see 1 Thessalonians 3:6-8).

4. Has there ever been a time when you've felt really lonely? Looking back, can you see God's purpose for that time?

5. What caution should we heed when moving from a church because of hurt or disillusionment? (See Psalm 101:5).

6. What are some fond memories you have of places you initially didn't enjoy? What are some things you appreciate about where you currently live?

7. Have you looked to God asking and expecting Him to fill your friendship needs? If so, how has He answered?

Chapter 4

Love at Arm's Length

On a cool, dank night in New Orleans on November 7, 1959, John Howard Griffin began a human experiment that would rock the foundations of American society. Through dyes and medication, John changed his skin color, thereby entering the social world of the Southern black. For seven weeks he toured the South, experiencing racial prejudice from the black man's perspective. The book he wrote about his discoveries, *Black Like Me,* has since become a classic on racial prejudice.

Prejudice—it's such a dirty word. We usually think of prejudice as the narrow, condescending stereotypes we carry in our minds. They are the attitudes that color how we respond to those around us. Prejudice can be directed toward different social groups whose values, lifestyles, religious beliefs, political perspectives or cultures we cannot respect. As *Black Like Me* so aptly illustrates, such thinking creates economic, political and relational barriers.

Yet barriers go up also when we think of a group more highly than we ought to. I call this reverse prejudice. And while reverse prejudice rarely creates economic or political barriers, it always creates social barriers.

Reverse Prejudice

My husband is involved in outreach, discipleship and the integration of new Christians into our local church. The toughest challenge of his ministry is not evangelism or discipleship. The toughest challenge is integration. Why? The answer lies in reverse prejudice.

The church can be a scary place. New Christians tend to huddle together like a group of frightened sheep. They wonder how they should act or react in their new environment. They watch others converse comfortably within established circles of friends, yet they don't always feel comfortable. Someone refers to a Bible reference. *Where is that found?* they wonder self-consciously. By the time they find the reference, the teacher has moved on to another passage. They tend to hold the experienced group (especially the leaders) in awe. The courageous ones may risk asking questions of the veteran, but most of them will likely keep their relationships at an arm's length.

Another place we see reverse prejudice is in the social gap between clergy and laity. I ran headlong into reverse prejudice in our first pastorate. Trying to be the proper pastor's wife I worked hard at having newcomers over for dinner. As a young mother of two preschoolers, I was eager also for the adult conversation the evening promised. All day I cleaned and re-cleaned the house (thanks to my toddlers). I did my best to prepare a nice meal. Always looking forward to the evening of visiting to come, I was unprepared for the disappointment ahead.

Our guests would arrive. The meal would be served, and conversation would begin. "Pastor," the husband or wife would ask, "I've had some questions about the end times. . . ." Off the conversation would go in pursuit of some religious topic. I listened patiently, tending to my children and the needs of our guests. Eventually dinner would end and we'd move to the living room. The topic of conversation would still be on some point of theology. There was no talk of other interests, our background or our children, even though we'd ask these questions of our guests. The conversation persisted between our guests and my husband on religious questions alone. In fact, I was hardly included in the conversation at all.

I couldn't completely understand it at first. Then we took a trip to the Midwest and I changed roles. My husband and I were in Omaha, Nebraska, at Christ Community Church to attend an Evangelism Explosion Clinic (a seminar designed to teach people to share their faith more effectively). I had been resistant to going. Learning to witness to total strangers sounded pretty scary to me. I would far rather have gone shopping, while my husband won the world to Christ. But God had other things in mind and I soon found myself flying toward Omaha, madly memorizing verses and illustrations for the intense six-day agenda ahead of us.

As if this wasn't enough stress, my husband and I planned to use our break times to look into the possibility of coming to Christ Community Church for a year of internship in outreach ministry. Minister of Outreach, Rev. Tom Stebbins, had mentored outreach interns before, but we would be the first couple to come from outside the Omaha area. This step presented a multitude of obstacles. Still, it seemed God was leading us in this direction.

During our clinic breaks we talked with the various elders on the governing board. As we perched nervously on couches in their living rooms, we told them that we felt God was directing us to move to Christ Community Church for a year. True, we had no place to live. True, Scott had no job. We just wanted to share our vision with them and ask them to pray about the possibility of allowing us to come. They listened intently and kindly. I let Scott do most of the talking. It still sounded pretty crazy to me. I couldn't imagine what it must have sounded like to them. "They must think we are led of the Lord, or totally nuts!"

my husband said grinning, as we drove to the next appointment. To be honest, I wasn't so sure which myself. Time would tell whether God was indeed leading us to take this step.

Hour by hour I lived through an incredibly stressful and pivotal week. Fortunately the EE Clinic had been pretty easy so far. The clinic included three nights of witnessing. Every evening was preceded by a dinner where we were assigned to a small visitation team. The first two nights my trainer told me I was simply to observe. *Fine by me*, I thought, somewhat relieved. The third night I knew I wouldn't get off so easy. That was the night the trainees were to share part of the gospel presentation.

I was tense as we arrived at dinner that night. But the tension was nothing compared with the utter terror that I'd soon feel when I was paired with my trainer who was not some unknown layman, but Bob Thune, senior pastor of Christ Community Church. The title SENIOR PASTOR stood out in neon capitals in my mind. I sat down in front of my tossed salad and couldn't swallow. Finally, I excused myself to the restroom, locked myself in a stall and poured out my heart to the Lord.

"God, I can't go through with this!" I prayed in panic and tears. "Of all the people to assign as my trainer! Bob Thune—the senior pastor of this gigantic church. I'll probably blow the gospel presentation and he'll look at me and say, 'There's no way we are letting your husband come as an intern if you can't even manage a decent witnessing opportunity!' "

Then God spoke to my heart in His still, small voice. "Cheryl, you are doing to Bob Thune just what you hate for people to do to you. He's simply My servant. You are putting him on a pedestal." Realizing what was happening, I almost laughed aloud. After all, prejudice is simply a matter of faulty perspective. Bob Thune might be the senior pastor of Christ Community Church, but he was also my brother in Christ, my equal before God. After a few minutes I dried my eyes, asked God once more to help me not say anything foolish and returned to enjoy my dinner and evening of team ministry.

This experience helped me to understand why my dinner guests in our logging town pastorate had asked only safe religious questions of my husband. What else could they talk to a pastor about when they were scared they'd say the wrong thing? As for the pastor's wife, who's to tell what subjects would be safe to talk with her about? They probably thought, *She must be somewhat religious. After all, she's married to the minister. I better settle for a nonthreatening discussion on religion.* And so, reverse prejudice kept us polite with one another, but far from being friends.

You may have experienced the same phenomenon in your workplace or when volunteering in your community. While trying to stay true to your identity as a Christian, you sense the walls of prejudice raised by those beside you. Rather than being a bridge to others, a Christian stance can become a formidable barrier. Is that wrong? After all, aren't we supposed to be different from the world? Are we inadvertently contributing to the mental pedestals we later resent? If so, how can we break through those barriers when we want to?

Is Reverse Prejudice Really Wrong?

Never has there been a greater proponent of civil rights than Jesus Christ. He reached out to touch and heal the alienated leper. He became known as the "friend of 'sinners' "—those despised by the core of Jewish society (Matthew 11:19). Women were elevated from their enslaved position to a place of dignity and mutual respect. Truly, no one shook the status quo like Jesus. Lest Jesus' disciples be deceived about His mission, He said:

> "Do not suppose that I have come to bring peace to the earth. I did not come to bring peace, but a sword. For I have come to turn 'a man against his father, a daughter against her mother, a daughter-in-law against her mother-in-law—a man's enemies will be the members of his own household.' " (10:34-36)

Jesus expected that the decision to follow Him would create barriers as well as destroy them. For some, the barriers would be incredibly painful. Jesus warned that families and marriages would split over a person's decision to follow Him. As the apostle Paul later wrote, "To the one we are the smell of death; to the other, the fragrance of life" (2 Corinthians 2:16). To be a true disciple of Christ is to live with the reality of prejudice. But is all prejudice the result of a Christian lifestyle?

The High Price of Pedestal Life

Zing! Cold spray that quickly warmed to scalding hot, hissed from the shower head pummeled my skin. Afterward, using a well-worn towel, I wiped off the water and dressed quickly in the chill of the empty locker room. A few minutes later I handed my damp towel to Sandy, the towel room attendant.

"Hey! You're Cheryl, aren't you?" she said eagerly as she returned my plastic student I.D. card.

"Yes," I responded cautiously.

"Well, I hear you're a Christian and that you're thinking of leaving here to go to Bible school?" she continued undeterred. "That's great! I'm a Christian and I want to go to Bible school, too!"

Thus began an incredible relationship between Sandy and me. As our friendship took wings, I learned that Sandy had just recently given her life to Christ. I also learned that she was the only distance runner on the newly formed women's track team. The coach had asked me to join the team as well, offering me a full scholarship if I would agree. After praying about it, I decided to accept the offer.

As the other distance runner on the team, Sandy and I were assigned workouts together daily. It was a perfect opportunity for discipleship. Nothing can be compared to those chilly autumn days we spent together. With the sunshine filtering through the pines and the river rapids rushing beside the road masking the sounds of the city, we jogged along sharing the joy of life and the wonders of Christ. Seldom did the miles seem long.

Sandy was so enthusiastic. She loved life, and she was on fire to tell the world about Jesus. I'm not sure who discipled who that year. I was certainly challenged by her uninhibited blend of life and faith. For my part, I tried very hard to present the image of a perfect Christian. I really wasn't a perfect Christian. What I tried to put across as Christianity was largely my own efforts, not God's enabling. What I didn't want Sandy to see was the uncertainties and struggles that were also part of my life.

Soon Sandy and I started praying together. We memorized Bible verses. Then we began to risk sharing our faith. After some urging by Sandy, I took my guitar along on our road trips. Sandy and I taught the team Christian choruses. One drippy morning in Seattle the team even sang a couple verses of "We Are One in the Spirit" to psych themselves for a tough cross-country meet!

By the time the spring season had come, one young woman had given her life to Christ. Another named Karen soon followed. Sandy rushed up to me, her face aglow with excitement. "Cheryl, you'll never believe what happened!" she bubbled. "Karen and I talked, and she's given her heart to Jesus." I was thrilled, of course. When I saw Karen at practice the next day, I mentioned her decision. Actually, I hardly needed to ask. Karen's whole person seemed to glow with fresh vitality.

"Sandy told me that you invited Christ into your life last week. Is that true?" I asked eagerly.

"That's right," she said smiling. Then almost apologetically she added, "I have been watching you for so long and wondering what made the difference. I wanted to come and ask you, but you seemed so different from me—so perfect. I didn't think you'd understand." That day my new baby sister in Christ taught me an unforgettable lesson: You can't minister from a pedestal. Being a Christian means living a righteous life, but it doesn't mean living a perfect life. People are watching us. They don't hunger for perfection. They hunger for reality. They want to know: how to find the courage to pick up the pieces of a broken heart and go on without bitterness; how to have a positive outlook in a world that seems so unpredictable;

how to be satisfied with what they have; how to suffer and yet not drown in despair. These quandaries have an answer in Christ, but it is visible only through our brokenness. Like a stained glass window, the blend of broken bits of color from the Christian's life yields the richest testimony when His light is allowed to shine through.

Not only does a pedestal life prevent a positive testimony, but it is dangerous as well. Prejudice has its roots in old-fashioned pride. And pride simply tempts us to try and be something we aren't.

Herod Agrippa I was a puppet king, ruling Palestine for the Roman government. After the Roman Emperor Caligula was murdered, Herod helped Claudius capture the throne. Claudius in turn rewarded Herod's loyalty, making him one of the most powerful governors of the Herodian dynasty (Lockyer 1986, 477-478). In simple terms, Herod Agrippa I was a pedestal personality. He was powerful, extravagant and he had connections with all the right people. If you were smart, you did what it took to stay in his favor.

Unfortunately, the coastal cities of Tyre and Sidon didn't play things politically correct. It isn't clear what the problem was, but the situation made Herod very angry. So when Herod left Jerusalem to attend the games being held in Caesarea, the people of Tyre and Sidon begged an audience to work things out (Marshall 1980,

211-212). Dressed in his royal robes, Herod entered the hall and began to address them. "This is the voice of a god, not a man," the crowds shouted (Acts 12:22). Herod's heart swelled with pride at their flattery. He was not just a good ruler, he was a godlike ruler! The crowds had placed him on a mental pedestal. Herod momentarily basked in the praise. Then the pedestal rocked, and he took a nasty fall. God humbled Herod because of his pride. Instead of ruling in awesome power and wisdom, Herod soon died of intestinal worms—not exactly a godlike ending.

A Cure for the Pedestal Mentality

Herod's death should act as a warning when we are tempted to place ourselves on a mental pedestal. Whether our own estimate places us above others, or we are there by the plaudits of others, we assume an unnatural position from which a fall is inevitable. The only solution for a pedestal mentality is given by Paul in Romans 12:3: "Do not think of yourself more highly than you ought, but rather think of yourself with sober judgment, in accordance with the measure of faith God has given you."

First, Paul places the negative warning before us—don't place yourself on a pedestal. Avoid sinful pride.

Second, hold on to a valid self-concept. Paul is not advocating the self-deprecating kind of talk that eats away at what God has created and enabled us to be. We are to hold our lives in healthy respect.

Third, we are to give all praise to God for what He does in and through us. All we are, all we ever will be, is because of Him. It is pride to lose sight of this reality.

Reversing Reverse Prejudice

Still, the predicament remains: If others hold us on some kind of pedestal, how can we break their misconceptions to establish an honest relationship? The answer is found in another man's reaction to praise.

Paul and Barnabas were preaching to a crowd in Lystra. A man who was lame from birth sat at the edge of the crowd listening intently as Paul spoke. Paul noticed him, and somehow discerned that this man had the faith to be healed. "Stand up on your feet!" Paul commanded (Acts 14:10). Immediately the lame man jumped to his feet and began walking. It was a miracle! Gasps of wonder, followed by excited murmurs, rippled through the crowd. The people were in awe of these foreigners with their new religion. Who were these men that could straighten bent limbs? What could it all mean? Had their mythical gods—Zeus and Hermes—revisited them in human form, as a popular myth said they had done once before?

Rumors flew from mouth to mouth, until myth was galvanized into reality. "The gods have come down to us in human form!" the townspeople exclaimed (Acts 14:11). The priest of the temple of Zeus quickly led oxen bedecked with festive wreaths to the city gates to sacrifice in Paul and Barnabas' honor (Marshall 1980, 236-238).

Because the people were speaking in their local dialect, it took Paul and Barnabas awhile to fully grasp the situation. When the rumor was revealed, however, the apostles reacted quickly. Tearing their garments (they did this to indicate their rejection of blasphemy—the idea that man could be like God), they rushed into the crowd. "Men, why are you doing this?" Paul demanded. "We too are only men, human like you. We are bringing you good news, telling you to turn from these worthless things to the living God, who made heaven and earth and sea and everything in them" (14:15). Yet even when he had finished speaking to the crowd, Paul and Barnabas still could hardly keep the people from worshiping them. Unlike Herod Agrippa, however, Paul and Barnabas did three things that helped them pull down the barriers of reverse prejudice.

Identification

First, they identified with the common man.

I remember once going to visit a neighbor. Lisa and I had talked over the fence from time to time, but I had never been over for tea as I was doing this morning. As I sat down at her kitchen table to talk, I noticed she seemed very tense. *The old reverse prejudice again,* I thought privately. *Well, this time I'm not going to let it get in the way!*

"Lisa," I said somewhat bravely. "I'll bet you are wondering what this pastor's wife is doing, coming over here to visit you like this, huh?"

She looked up at me, somewhat shocked at my frankness. "Well, yes, I was kind of wondering," she admitted sheepishly.

"Lisa, I came over just to visit. So many people hold me at arm's length because I'm a pastor's wife. It's like they are afraid I'll hit them over the head with a big Bible or something. Lisa, I just want to visit with you about day-to-day things like anybody else would."

The tension evaporated from the room. I was a real person after all. True, my husband was a pastor, but that didn't make Lisa my next "project." And wonder of wonders, I had needs too! That day Lisa and I put away my pedestal and I began learning about a fascinating woman whom I would call both neighbor and friend.

Perspective

Second, Paul and Barnabas maintained their perspectives. God alone is worthy of worship. It sounds so simple. Who would really be so arrogant to think of himself as a god? Yet pride is subtle. We are all too easily deceived into worshiping our own egos. Have you ever sat back at a Christian sharing time and wondered who was really getting the glory? I can remember sharing glowing testimonies about leading others to faith in Christ, but having the spotlight on my soul-winning ability, not the Holy Spirit's. If we find ourselves isolated by reverse prejudice or scorn in these situations, we have only ourselves to blame. The truth is that all we have, all we are or ever will be, is because of Him. Our only honor is to do His bidding.

A Word of Restraint

Third, we need to restrain others from exalting us. Even after identifying with the people and restoring their perspective on God, Paul and Barnabas still had to work to keep the people of Lystra from worshiping them. Man has always liked to make little gods in his own image to look up to, but not be threatened by. These gods are more popularly called heroes. If God places you in a position of influence, you'll become someone's hero, if you let them make you a hero. Resisting the role of hero means you make identification and right perspective a way of life.

Recently, I was talking with a friend. In the course of our conversation I shared with her some answers to prayer God had provided. One such answer was the opportunity to write this book. "Wow," she responded. "I've got a famous friend!"

Instinctively I sensed a pedestal and drew back. "I don't know," I responded hesitantly. "Maybe I'll be famous someday, but I hope I never go around thinking about being famous."

"Well," she said laughing, "I'm sure the Lord will remind you quickly if you make that mistake." The Lord may remind me, but I'd rather He wouldn't have to.

Proverbs 16:18 says, "Pride goes before destruction, a haughty spirit before a fall." That sounds pretty painful. Instead, pray for humility to mark your character so when people see you, they'll see Jesus. Sure, it's all right to accept another person's word of thanks or praise with a simple reply such as, "Thank you for sharing that with me." "I'm so glad to hear how God has used me in your life." "Praise the Lord! Isn't it amazing how He can meet our needs through one another."

We should be quick to encourage one another to faithful service, but we must be careful not to encourage others to make us the focus of their praise. God is the end focus. We are just channels. When the praise seems to be directed exclusively at us, we need to offer a gentle word of restraint.

Take It from Bear-Bear

Soon after my daughter was born, a package arrived in the mail. Inside was a big, cuddly teddy bear soon to be known as Bear-Bear. He was my daughter's constant companion who went everywhere with us. I've backtracked countless miles to retrieve him when he's been accidently left behind. I've repaired him when his stitches came loose or his stuffing needed to be replaced. Then finally Bear-Bear's fur began to fall out. Now he occupies a special place atop my daughter's dresser, far from the destructive rub of daily life.

What makes the difference between people who are loved at arm's length and friendships held close? I think it's partly what worked for Bear-Bear. You see, Bear-Bear was a very unpretentious teddy. He came from a well known toy company, but Sierra didn't know that. At first, he was bigger than she was. But Bear-Bear didn't make Sierra feel small. As time passed he got shabbier and shabbier, but somehow that only seemed to make him more precious.

Like Bear-Bear, people who want intimate friendships don't let preconceived ideas stand in their way. They don't make others feel small. Instead they make themselves approachable, vulnerable and real. In the end, they are loved not for what they are, but for whom they have become. In fact, if Bear-Bear could speak, I think he'd tell you that love at arm's length is hardly love at all. It's worth getting your fur rubbed off if that's what it takes to be real.

Making It Yours

1. How does reverse prejudice differ from regular prejudice, or do you think there's a difference?

2. Have you ever been frustrated by others' prejudicial attitudes toward you? Share your experience. How did you resolve the situation?

3. Jesus said that prejudice will be part of our lives as Christians (see Matthew 10:34-36). Does this mean that all prejudicial barriers need to be accepted without question?

4. What are the two dangers of trying to live our lives on some kind of pedestal?

5. What is the biblical cure for a pedestal mentality? (see Romans 12:3).

6. What are three steps we can take to reverse prejudice? (zee Acts 14:8-18).

Chapter 5

Of a Kindred Spirit

In her delightful Victorian novel *Anne of Green Gables*, author L.M. Montgomery captures the hope of every human heart as Anne confesses her longing for a special friend. "A bosom friend," Anne tells her guardian, Marilla. "An intimate friend, you know—a really kindred spirit to whom I can confide my inmost soul. I've dreamed of meeting her all my life. I never really supposed I would, but so many of my loveliest dreams have come true all at once that perhaps this one will too" (Montgomery [1908] 1935, 57).

Like Anne, have you also dreamed of having a special friend—someone you can love and share your life with unreservedly? Perhaps you've been fortunate enough to have such a friend. Maybe you are married to him. Maybe you wish you were.

What separates those who are friends from the select few who become kindred spirits? Does intimacy rely on chance—that mystical, emotional chemistry that sometimes happens between people? Are there steps that we can take to promote intimacy in relationships? Can we tell which friendships have potential to be close and which do not?

Levels of Relationship

Understanding intimacy begins with understanding the nature of the relationship we are embracing. To this end, several authors have compared relationships to something like an archery target.

Acquaintances make up the exterior circle. These are people we meet at church, soccer

practice, school functions, etc. We know their names, perhaps where they work and how many children they have. We rarely spend time with them outside of the settings where our paths cross. For a multitude of reasons, they seldom evolve into close friends.

Friends comprise the next level. They have come to mean more to us than acquaintances. They are individuals we enjoy and with whom we have shared experiences. They may be co-workers who eat lunch with us, someone who joins us for a movie or sits with us at church. We share more personal information with friends. While acquaintances are given facts, our friends are trusted with our opinions and feelings. We allow friends to share a measure of our lives.

Close friends make up the next level of relationship. Jesus had three such friends: Peter, James and John. Few people have more than three close friends. Some people, sadly, have none. Relationships of this depth require a continual investment in time and energy. They expose not only our opinions and feelings, but our vulnerabilities as well. At this level, the title "friend" is undergirded with a costly love and enduring loyalty. And while friends may come and go, close friendships tend to touch our lives for a lifetime.

Our *immediate family* makes up the next level. We don't typically think of our children as friends. As the cartoon character Charlie Brown says, "You can choose your friends but you can't choose your relatives" (Block 1980, 209). Still, our relationship with our children is definitely an intimate one. In fact, nowhere are we invited to practice friendship in a purer form. For what is friendship but voluntarily sharing your life with someone, comforting and confronting them in love, giving and forgiving unconditionally and, at times, asking forgiveness? Raising children calls us to develop and practice the basics of friendship because they know us at our best and at our worst. If the elements of Christian friendship become a way of life, most family relationships mature and endure through the years.

Your relationship with your *spouse* should ideally be your closest earthly friendship. After all, no other relationship is so honored by God as to become an example of His love for the Church. No other relationship is described by Him as the remaking of two identities into one. In no other relationship has He commanded complete mutual authority over one another's lives, or blessed with sexual expression. The relationship of marriage, as God intends it, is unique. Sadly, many married couples have not been able to enjoy marriage as a friendship. While they may have worked out a reasonable balance of power and have contained their sexual expression within this relationship, their emotional investments have all been made at lower levels. For them marriage is a relationship, but it has not become a friendship. I firmly believe that when Christ said, "What God has joined together, let man not separate" (Matthew 19:6). He was including emotional separation as well. God's plan is that friendship with our mate should hone our lives and warm our hearts.

The last level of friendship is a spiritual one—our friendship with *God*. Are you God's friend? Do you take the time to talk to Him, to share with Him your praises as well as your heartaches? Are you ever quiet long enough for Him to relate to you? God desires our worship, but He longs for our friendship as well. An old Arabian proverb says:

A friend is one
To whom one may pour
Out all the contents
Of one's heart,
Chaff and grain together
Knowing that the
Gentlest of hands
Will take and sift it,
Keep what is worth keeping
And with a breath of kindness
Blow the rest away.
(Block 1980, 199)

God intends for us to have such a relationship with Him. He longs to speak to us intimately. He uses a "voice" that speaks to the heart and sometimes the words are straight from Scripture. Such a friendship will transform a life. Moses had such a relationship with God. Exodus 33:11 says: "The LORD would speak to Moses face to face, as a man speaks with his friend." The result was that Moses' face glowed with the glory of God. In fact, he was so radiant after spending time with God, that Moses had to veil his face to keep from scaring the other Israelites (see Exodus 34:29-35). Yet I wonder how many friends God has had since Moses' day. Is God your friend? If so, you've embraced the most intimate friendship of all.

Applying the Archery Target

Identifying relationships on this archery target diagram helps in several ways. First, it helps regulate the emotional investment. Knowing that someone could possibly become a close friend is motivation to make opportunities for that relationship to grow. It may require bypassing opportunities to be with others and involve the risk of sharing more with that person than with more impersonal friends.

Second, identifying a relationship helps to temper expectations. For example, a close friend remembers your birthday. Conversely, it is a surprise when an acquaintance does. If a spouse forgets a birthday, feelings are wounded. The difference lies in the level of the relationship and the expectations that go with it. The more intimate the relationship, the greater the responsibilities involved.

Third, this diagram charts relational priorities that God blesses. Our relationship with God is our most important friendship. Our relationships with our spouse and children are next. Commitments to close friends, friends and acquaintances complete the list in a descending order of importance. It seems simple enough, yet few allow God's plan for relationships to guide their lives. Increasing family problems and rising divorce rates show that many people consistently disregard God's plan for relationships and live to regret it.

But life is seldom as simple as a diagram. The balance of relationships is continually changing. One week will be busy with friends. The next week the kids will need more time and attention. One evening may be scheduled for just husband and wife to do something together. Without being overly introspective, the question is: Do your investments in time and energy match up with God's plan? When they don't, you are headed for heartache.

Still, identifying our relationships is only a start. The questions remain: What is the recipe for relational intimacy? What makes a friendship become a cherished kindred spirit?

The Making of a Kindred Spirit

I'm not sure anyone has fully answered this question. In her book, *The Friendships of Women*, Dee Brestin observed: "A best friendship begins, often, with the same sort of feelings that lovers feel when meeting. We notice something and are pulled" (Brestin 1988, 102). It's true. There is an element of mystery about the making of a kindred spirit.

Generally, we are closest to those who are most like us. Children play with children and often distinguish their friendships according to grade level. Adults are drawn closest to those within their peer group, economic strata or political alliance. The more common threads that knit us together, the stronger the friendship.

In his autobiographical book, *A Severe Mercy*, Sheldon Vanauken tells how common interests yielded a rich, romantic depth to his marriage. Early in the book he shares their philosophy for intimacy:

> We shall create a thousand strands, great and small, that will link us together. Then we shall be so close that it would be impossible—unthinkable—for either of us to suppose that we could ever recreate such closeness with anyone else. And our trust in each other will not only be based on love and loyalty but on the fact of a thousand sharings—a thousand strands twisted into something unbreakable. (Vanauken 1977, 27)

Such was true for Sheldon and Davy Vanauken—at least initially. When Davy Vanauken made her decision to follow Christ, she stepped away from her husband's stance of atheism. Doing so meant Davy no longer shared her husband's unbelief. Sheldon was devastated by his wife's decision. He was jealous of her relationship with Christ. Yet in time through Davy's faithful prayer, her changed life and the witness of a friend, Sheldon also gave his heart to Christ.

But although united in creed, their commitment to Christ differed vastly. Sheldon wrote:

> I wanted life itself, the colour and fire and loveliness of life. And Christ now and then, like a loved poem I could read when I wanted to. I didn't want us to be swallowed up in God. . . . For Davy, to live was Christ. . . . She simply wanted God— almost totally. . . . She loved me, she loved our sharing; but, ultimately, all there was to share was Christ and His service. (Vanauken 1977, 134-135)

The difference threatened anew to shipwreck their marriage. Sheldon toyed with an emotional attachment to another woman. Even though Davy knew what was happening, she continued steadfast in her commitment to Christ, always praying faithfully for her husband. In time Davy's prayers were answered, and Sheldon followed Davy into a deeper walk with Christ. Theirs became a companionship not compromised by God, but completed in Him. The result was a marriage friendship held sweet and strong until Davy's final dying breath.

Faith in Christ can divide (Matthew 10:34-36) or unite a relationship (Galatians 3:26-28). Only a common bond in Jesus Christ provides for intimacy in relationships like nothing else.

Incredible obstacles such as illness or loss can be spanned through a shared commitment to Christ. A career missionary once shared with me that her closest friends have often been missionaries from other countries. She admitted the differences in cultures and backgrounds required her to stretch to make the friendships work. Without Christ, the friendships would have been impossible. Because of Him, a rich, loving bonding had taken place.

Such testimonies are not surprising. Many say they have never experienced such intimate friendship outside of Christian circles. When Christ reigns in our hearts, He gives us an unconditional love for one another. If we recognize God's divine appointment of friendships within our lives through common interests and a shared commitment to Christ, it is almost impossible for close friendships not to grow.

Does this mean then that Christians are never lonely? Could we put up billboards that read: "Come to Christ and Discover Close Friends?" If only life were that simple. But sharing common threads and faith are only part of the mysterious mix that makes for intimate friendship.

You Can Count on Me!

Loyalty sometimes seems as antiquated as medieval chivalry. Prenuptial agreements protect the estates of the rich and famous should they divorce. Some businesses are built on cutthroat competition. Even the local church can hardly hold its own against mega churches offering every conceivable ministry and entertainment. Loyalty has become a rare commodity today.

Of course, a lack of loyalty is often the result of a selfish attitude. Like an early frost it can nip the best of friendships and keep them from blossoming into a rich experience. Yet where loyalty endures, its fragrance is unforgettable.

Carol and Nancy met in Bangkok, Thailand, as Nancy and her husband helped the new missionary couple get settled into their apartment. Nancy laughingly recalls how their friendship began. "I had some chocolate, but I didn't want the kids to see it. So I motioned for Carol to come over behind the refrigerator. Sharing that chocolate in secret is how our friendship began." It was a sweet start, but it takes more than chocolate to cement kindred spirits.

In the years that passed, their friendship continued to grow. When both Nancy and Carol sent their children off to a mission school in

Dalat, the common heartache drew them even closer. Then came the day that Nancy and her husband returned to the States to minister. Tears were shed over that parting as well.

With half a world between them, it would have been easy to neglect such a friendship. But Nancy and Carol were kindred spirits. Although they were miles apart, their hearts were committed to one another in Christ's love. When Carol was diagnosed with breast cancer a year later, Nancy wanted nothing more than to be at her friend's side. How was such a trip possible? Where could she find the money for the airfare? What about child care for her three boys?

Soon after Carol's diagnosis a fierce hailstorm swept through Nancy's neighborhood which caused damage that could be submitted as an insurance claim. As her husband collected the insurance settlement he said, "I think this is your money to go to Bangkok." Nancy had cleared the first barrier.

Then when Nancy's Sunday school class learned of her situation they took care of the rest. "If it's only child care that is keeping you," they said, "we can handle that." The class wrote up a schedule for caring for the children, and Nancy was on her way to Thailand.

The two women spent two precious weeks together. Carol's husband would later comment, "That visit meant so much to Carol. I believe it was one of the things that brought her through. She did much better after that. You might say, Nancy saved Carol's life."

Thankfully, we serve a God who has designed friendship. He longs to use us to touch one another's lives. In so doing, we touch the world (see John 13:34-35).

Love and loyalty walk hand in hand. The fervent lovers in the Song of Songs cried:

Place me like a seal over your heart,
　like a seal on your arm;
for love is as strong as death,
　its jealousy unyielding as the grave . . .
Many waters cannot quench love;
　rivers cannot wash it away.
If one were to give
　all the wealth of his house for love,
　it would be utterly scorned. (8:6-7)

Can your friendship be trusted? Will you be there to share the joys? Will you weep with me in my sorrow? These are the questions an intimate friendship asks. Loyalty may seem old fashioned, but it can make the difference between friendships we like and those we love.

I Just Wanted You to Know

Empathy is another ingredient in the mix for intimacy. The concept springs originally from the Greek word *empatheia*, meaning affection. The idea here is to listen to another with affection. We can talk with others about many things, even personal issues. It is those that lis-

ten empathetically, however, that we feel closest to.

The spring of 1990 found our family in
Omaha, Nebraska. Having moved from a
three-bedroom home in Washington to a two-
bedroom apartment in Omaha, we had lots of
"stuff" stored in a separate garage building.
Our Christmas decorations were in there along
with all of Scott's power tools, garden tools and
his pastoral library. We were only planning to
live in Omaha one year and a lot of things
wouldn't be needed before the next move. We
were grateful the apartment complex offered
ample storage.

Summer arrived with crackling electrical
storms and ear-splitting thunder. The cicadas
buzzed in the treetops. And the hot, humid air
wrapped itself around everything in a sticky
embrace. By August life outdoors had slowed
to a crawl. It was too hot for anything to
move—anything, that is, except fire.

"Scott, the garage is on fire!" I yelled. Scoop-
ing up the kids, we pounded down the stair-
well and into the sweltering August heat. Gray
smoke poured from under the eaves of the
parking garage. Soon a column of fire burst
through the roof. Fanned by a hot summer
wind the flames whipped into a raging fire
storm. Five fire engines responded to the call.
The heat was so intense that several firefighters
buckled from heat exhaustion. Taillights on
nearby cars melted and dribbled over blistered

enamel. Double pane windows in nearby buildings expanded with the heat and burst. In the end, the fire crew settled for simply containing the blaze. Scott and I stood and watched. In little over an hour the 100-foot parking garage had burned to the ground with all our belongings in it.

If you've been through a loss like this, you'll understand our overwhelming sense of despair those first few days. We struggled with the obvious financial loss of our possessions as well as the sentimental value of many items. In the days following I spent hours sifting through charred photo albums trying to salvage our memories. Intellectually, I knew God was still in control of our situation, but emotionally I felt raw and violated.

After several days a friend called. "How are you doing?" Teresa asked. I didn't really know Teresa very well. We had done a few things together. Still our young friendship seemed to hold potential to grow closer. So rather than give a routine response, I made myself vulnerable.

"I'm doing pretty well," I said cautiously. "It's just such an overwhelming loss. How will we ever replace all that?"

"I've got a verse for you," she said quickly. Then Teresa read Job 1:21—"Naked I came from my mother's womb, and naked I will depart." She continued, "You know, Cheryl, you can't take it with you anyway. Just keep your eyes on the Lord."

Teresa was a young Christian. Passing along a Bible verse was her way of trying to minister to me. Because I understood Teresa's intentions, I curtailed my initial response to her counsel, but inside I felt anger, not encouragement. It is true that we can't take the things of life with us into eternity, but it certainly hurts to lose them in the here and now. If Teresa had taken a moment to imagine what I was facing, she would have understood that. While she did listen and was concerned, she failed to be empathetic. Instead of receiving a verbal hug, I had to settle for a lecture. Although our friendship remained intact, it isn't surprising that I was hesitant to lay my emotions bare before Teresa again.

If good communication includes identifying with another's heartache, it also includes sharing our own feelings. Why is it that we find it so hard to tell friends that we love them? I suppose we are afraid of being misunderstood. No doubt we also fear rejection. So while we enjoy another's company, the time never seems right to say how we've grown to care for them.

The final church service before we moved from our first pastorate was incredibly emotional. I told someone, "It was like attending my own funeral." Friends and acquaintances alike hugged us, crying openly and telling us what we had meant to them. My heart was broken as well. In fact, the last day I stepped aside with my closest friend and said brokenly: "I

love you. I just thought you should know that."
I guess my tears said the rest.

How foolish it is to wait so long to express
our feelings. As I drove the long miles to
Omaha, I determined never to put off saying
until tomorrow loving words that could be said
today. How many people long to hear the
words "I love you" or "I'm proud of you" from
a father or mother? Many never heard those
words. Mom or Dad just never got around to it,
and then they were gone. Certainly we don't
want to go around gushing over everyone. Too
much of a good thing is just as bad as too little.
But we are all a little like puppy dogs. We long
for encouragement, a loving pat on the back or
a verbal hug from time to time. When such
words pass between friends, they become
treasured gifts. As Proverbs 16:24 says, "Pleasant words are a honeycomb, sweet to the soul
and healing to the bones."

Remember When

It is almost impossible to build intimate
friendships without the passage of time. I suppose that is why many people recall childhood
friends when they think of kindred spirits.
Childhood often holds friends together with
years of memories. "Remember when we tried
to water ski behind a row boat?" a friend reminds me. (Yes, I really tried that.) "I wonder
whatever happened to that boy at the lake resort that had a crush on you." I groan as I recall

the summer I spent on the run from Jim. We both laugh at the shared recollections.

The passage of time, spiced with memory building experiences, transforms friends into kindred spirits. As children, life throws us together in many settings—school, club, church, neighborhood. In the course of life and play, time passes and memories are stored in our heart.

As we move on to young adulthood, our paths often separate. If we are able to remain in contact, close childhood friendships can carry on into our adult years. Yet for most, life moves us on. Once we settle again, however, we can nurture new friendships toward intimacy. We do this by sharing memory building experiences. Granted, as our paths cross, some of these will happen of their own accord.

Other memories take special planning. Recently, I was to speak at a retreat on the same weekend that a friend's son was to be married. Because of another conflict, I had missed her daughter's wedding a few years earlier. I decided there was no way I was going to miss her son's wedding. After talking with the coordinator of the retreat, we worked out a schedule that allowed me to share that special evening with my friend and still make the retreat. That evening is a memory Mary and I will always share, but it took planning to make it happen.

Memory building experiences also yield intimacy with your children. In our family we have Pal-to-Pal dates when either my husband, Scott, or I do something special with one of our children. The "dates" are not extravagant but are often memorable. Every Christmas Sierra and I recall the first time we went to see an amateur production of the *Nutcracker Ballet*. It wasn't all that professional, but she was enthralled. Together we shared an evening of romantic fantasy we'll both hold dear forever.

Other Pal-to-Pals have been simpler yet. One morning Michael and I drove to a nearby construction site where heavy equipment was belching diesel fumes. Climbing up on a pile of logs, we spent several hours watching those big noisy machines carve out a new street. That, too, was a shared experience that built intimacy. Acts of kindness are another way to build memories. A note, card or occasional surprise just to demonstrate your love creates a warm remembrance that is cherished long afterward.

One autumn day someone jammed the drawer shut on Scott's tool box. My husband is pretty handy, but by the time he had unjammed the drawer, the tool box was ruined. Admittedly, it seemed like just an old battered tool box to me. But I could tell having it bent and broken was very discouraging to Scott. The kids and I all felt badly about Dad's loss. Then I noticed a flyer advertising a sale on tool boxes at the local hardware store. I had been saving some spending money. It wasn't enough to replace the nice tool box Scott had lost, but enough to purchase a new one. That evening I waited until Scott left for a meeting. Then the kids and I quickly went out and purchased the new red, shiny tool box. Back at home, we left the box inside the back door with a note:

> I'm terribly sorry your tool box was ruined. I know this isn't the same. Exchange it if you like. But you do so many handy things around the house, I wanted you to have a good one. Love, Cheryl

Imagine Scott's surprise to find a big package waiting for him when he came home. Ordinarily, tool boxes aren't on my shopping list. I could have used that spending money in many other ways, but never could I have reaped the investment in intimacy that buying a new tool box brought to our friendship. The gift did more than meet a need; it expressed my friendship in a tangible way. The experience turned a heartache into a warm memory. And, no, he didn't exchange it.

The Things We Can't Say

I think it is interesting that touch was an important part of Jesus' public ministry. Jesus touched nearly every person that He healed. He gathered the Jewish children in His arms and blessed them. On the night before His betrayal, Jesus knelt and tenderly washed the disciples' feet. Neither did Jesus rebuke the prostitute who braved ridicule to anoint Him with perfume, wash His feet with her tears and dry them with her hair.

Touch is a powerful communicator because it says what words can't. Leprosy was a dreaded contagious disease. Because there was no cure, lepers had to live apart from the rest of society (see Leviticus 13:45-46). A leper also had "to wear mourning clothes, leave his hair in disorder, keep his beard covered and cry 'Unclean! Unclean!' so everyone could avoid him" (Lockyer 1986, 643). Knowing this, consider the impact of Jesus' encounter with a leper in Matthew, Chapter 8.

Jesus had just finished a period of profound teaching we call the Sermon on the Mount. As He left the area, a leper approached and bowed down before Jesus. "Lord," he said, "if you are willing, you can make me clean" (8:2).

The leprous man believed in Jesus' healing power. It was Jesus' love that was in question. Would Jesus command healing, or would He send him back into leprous isolation? Verse three gives us Jesus' response: "Jesus reached out his hand and touched the man. 'I am willing,' he said. 'Be clean!' " (8:3).

Imagine the power of that gesture. Going against all social norms—going against the Law itself—Jesus demonstrated His love and acceptance through a simple touch.

We live in a world starved for affection. Unfortunately, our society has twisted affection with so many sexual messages that many are afraid to touch another person for fear of being misunderstood. If we haven't grown up in an affectionate family, touching another person can seem wrong or awkward. Some people fear their own hunger for affection will overwhelm them and their affection will evolve into inappropriate gestures.

Yet while all these are healthy concerns, touch still remains a strong link in bonding kindred spirits. Nothing encourages like a gentle hand on the shoulder of one bowed with discouragement. A warm embrace for a friend somehow lightens the load or shares their joy. There's a subtle expression of unity and devotion when our family holds hands for prayer around the dinner table. Affection adds a silent warmth to relationships.

Here Are a Few Suggested Guidelines Regarding Affection

1. Never touch someone in an inappropriate or sexually suggestive manner.

2. Don't over use affection so that the gesture becomes meaningless.

3. Don't seek affection that should be supplied by your spouse.

4. Do cultivate expressions of affection within your marriage. Don't save touch just for sex.

5. Don't embarrass another person through your affection. Our kids appreciate our hugs, but not in front of their friends. Respect the preferences of another.

6. Do touch another person to communicate God's comfort and acceptance. This is what Jesus did. We can confidently follow His example.

The beautiful Marilyn Monroe had a difficult childhood. Following her parents' divorce, Marilyn's mother became institutionalized in a mental hospital. As a result Marilyn was shuffled from one foster home to another. When a reporter asked Marilyn if she ever felt loved by the families in those homes, she responded: "Once, when I was about seven or eight. The woman I was living with was putting on makeup, and I was watching her. She was in a happy mood, so she reached over and patted my cheeks with her rouge puff. . . . For that moment, I felt loved by her" (Smalley 1986, 48).

The world is filled with love-hungry people like Marilyn Monroe. They may seem glamorous on the outside, but inside they ache for an affirming touch. Some may be your friends.

Let's Pray

"Praying with a friend bonds you faster than anything I know" (Brestin 1988, 88). I agree with Dee Brestin—there's nothing like praying together to create depth in a friendship. One person even told me, "Prayer can be an excuse to have a friendship." Excuse or not, since I've learned to make prayer an essential part of my friendships, I can't imagine relating without it. In fact every time we move, I pray, "Lord send me a prayer partner." It goes without saying that the person He sends will become a close friend. Praying together creates depth because it easily incorporates the elements of intimacy already mentioned. For a good prayer partnership to work there must be a commitment to pray together regularly, and to hold in confidence sensitive requests. Praying together requires the deep sharing of needs and feelings. Humble honesty and empathy are key ingredients. As time passes, you are bound together by the thrill of watching God answer your prayers.

One winter afternoon I sat down to visit with Carole and Sandy. These women had been praying together for 16 years. What a thrill it was to hear their testimony. At times their voices choked with emotion. God had been so good. Carole recalled the time Sandy's son was waiting for a bone marrow transplant. He was quite weak with a chromosomal abnormality. All of the doctors concurred that his condition would soon develop into full-blown leukemia. The transplant seemed his only chance. But Sandy and Carole had been praying faithfully that God would heal Nathan. The day of the surgery, the doctor did one final test. The results? The chromosomal abnormalities had disappeared! Nathan had been healed. Yes, God does answer prayer. Sharing the burden and the answers builds memories that last forever.

And what is more natural than to hold hands in prayer, or to embrace a friend that has bared her soul? Praying together allows us to know how our friend is hurting. It makes us sensitive to God's direction as to how we might minister. One time I was sharing with someone what having a prayer partner has meant in my life. "I love her," I said. "I love her because through prayer she holds my life in her hands."

Picture two climbers scaling the face of a mountain. That's what a prayer partnership is like. While one steps out in faith, the other anchors them both to the Rock in faithful prayer. Then the tide of life changes and it's the other person's turn to climb. And should either friend fall, the other will call him back to God through loving, godly counsel. Through prayer partnerships we hold each other's lives in our hands.

Another reason praying together breeds kindred spirits is given to us by Christ himself. "For where two or three come together in my name," Jesus said, "there am I with them" (Matthew 18:20). Mysterious as it is, Jesus is present with us in a deeper way when we pray with another. This truth has been experienced by many of the prayer partners I've talked with.

One said, "You know you are sitting there, but you just *feel* Christ's presence."

I remember one such time when I was struggling over some doctrinal questions. Mary and I brought my search before the Lord. It was much like other times we had prayed together, yet this time I sensed the Lord's presence in a powerful way. It was almost as if I could have reached out and touched Him. He was there, bonding our friendship, receiving our worship and ministering to our hearts.

Praying and praising our Lord together is a taste of what heaven will be like. We will live in Christ's presence together, our voices raised in His praises. In fact, when you think about it, praying with a prayer partner is a little piece of heaven itself.

Do you long for a kindred spirit friendship? You needn't leave the development of such a relationship to chance. Begin by asking God to send you a prayer partner—then watch for His answer. Don't be in a hurry. Allow the relationship to unfold. You may have a few false starts but persevere. The friend God chooses may not at first seem whom you'd expect. Use the principles here and you may discover as Anne Shirley did that "kindred spirits are not so scarce as I used to think. It's splendid to find out there are so many of them in the world" (Montgomery [1908] 1935, 159).

Making It Yours

1. Think about the different levels of relationships in your life. How does your investment in time and energy match the priorities God has established? What changes do you need to make? What plan do you have for implementing those changes?

2. Read Ruth 1. Naomi was close to both her daughters-in-law. What allowed one relationship to deepen and the other to fade? How many of the elements of a kindred spirit friendship can you find in Ruth's friendship with Naomi?

3. Read Proverbs 20:5. What does it mean when it says, "but a man of understanding draws them out"? Why is it easier to bare your heart to a kindred spirit than someone else?

4. Do you find it difficult to put your feelings for another person into words? If so, why? Is there anyone that needs to know that they are special to you? How would God have you respond?

5. Do you need to build memories with your spouse, your children or a friend? What are some ways you might begin building those memories?

6. Use the following references to study how Jesus used touch (or allowed it) to minister to others.

Mark 10:13-16.   Luke 8:40-50.
Luke 5:12-13.   Luke 10:30-37.
Luke 7:36-50.   John 13:3-5.

7. Read and reflect on these verses about prayer:

1 Samuel 12:23. Matthew 18:20. James 5:16.

What are some reasons close friends should also be praying friends? Can you think of other reasons?

8. Do you need to ask God for a prayer partner?

Chapter 6

When It Isn't Working

I just don't know what to do," I complained to my husband. "Every time I go over to Sue's, she spends our entire visit griping. I want to reach out and encourage her, but I come away emotionally drained. I'm not sure my visits are doing either of us any good."

Have you ever had a promising friendship turn sour? What did you do? How did you handle the growing tension in your relationship? In the case above, I did what many people do in such situations. I began distancing myself from Sue. Instead of visiting weekly, as I'd originally hoped to do, I began occasionally substituting a phone call. I also tried to bring up positive subjects to talk about. In the end, Sue read my distance as rejection. One day when I called to visit, she responded abruptly and hung up on me. I didn't bother to call back.

You may have encountered a similar relational fiasco. Have you ever had a friend who is always gushing about how close you are when you rarely have a significant conversation? What about the friend who wants you exclusively to herself, almost demanding time and attention? Occasionally I've had friends who have challenged my walk with Christ by urging me to compromise on issues I feel strongly about. Either they feel I'm not conservative enough, or that I'm being too conservative because I've chosen a different stand.

As Christians, how should we respond when a relationship just isn't working? Are there warning signals we can use to identify problem relationships before we get too deeply involved? Worse yet, are we unknowingly relating in a way that will lead to problems? Thankfully, the Bible offers some practical counsel.

Warning #1: The Subtle Hiss of Compromise

Evening descends at our house with the routine noises of family life—conversation and dinner preparation, the clatter of dinner dishes and the subdued scratching of a pencil scribbling homework. Finally, after the kids are tucked in bed, I tune the radio to an easy listening station, grab a good book and stretch out on the sofa for some well-deserved relaxation. If only life were perfect. Inevitably my radio station drifts and a slight static hiss begins to compete with the melodies. It's never much of a disturbance at first. Often I try to ignore it, but then it seems to get a bit worse. Finally, I can ignore the static no longer and I'm in front of the radio doing my best to tune in a clear signal.

Like the slight static hiss on the radio, compromise can be the first warning signal of a friendship that is going astray. Here then are some typical symptoms of compromise hiss:

Your friend begins pressuring you to do something that you don't feel right about.

Your friend consistently offers counsel that seems contrary to Scripture.

Your friend's lifestyle is increasingly characterized by ungodliness. (See Galatians 5:19-21.)

Personally, compromising on my Christian values with friends has never produced anything but remorse and regret. It has certainly never—NEVER—led to a deeper friendship and here's why.

Let's say you and a friend decide to attend a movie together. Although you anticipate the movie you've chosen to be full of immorality and/or violence and sense the Holy Spirit's prick of warning, you decide to ignore Him.

"I think it will be a good show," you say to your friend encouragingly. "Besides, I need to get out of the house, and there aren't really many good movies around anyway. This is probably the best of what is available. Let's go."

Two Cokes and a bucket of popcorn later, you and your friend have seen the latest Hollywood version of passion and violence. It wasn't an ethical movie, but listen to your conversation as you walk to the car:

"That was a pretty good show, huh?"
"Well, that one scene was pretty steamy."
"It wasn't nearly as violent as I thought it would be. What did you think?"
"It could have been worse."

This kind of compromise can lead in only one of two directions—to rationalizations like this one, or to repentance.

"I'm sorry. We'll have to be more choosy the next time we pick a movie."

When compromising friendships are continually propped up with rationalizations, our credibility as Christians suffers and our walk with Christ is hindered. Christian friendships don't flourish under these conditions and the flame of friendship can be snuffed out as a result.

While occasionally watching a bad movie with a friend probably won't shipwreck your relationship, some compromises can lead a friend into serious problems. In Romans 14, Paul challenges the self-centered thinking that compromises involve. "None of us lives to himself alone," Paul wrote.

Instead, make up your mind not to put any stumbling block or obstacle in your brother's way. . . . Let us therefore make

every effort to do what leads to peace and
to mutual edification. (14:7, 13-19)

It would be interesting to know how many
alcoholics began their drinking with friends.
The same questions could be asked regarding
countless other addictions. In such cases, the
person once called friend has become an enemy.

If you or your friend are continually compromising your Christian values, beware. The Bible
calls us to respect and build up one another.
Tearing down values in the name of fun is not
Christian fellowship. Such a friendship is
headed in the wrong direction.

Warning #2: Manipulation—The Twisted Motive

Another killer of friendships is manipulation.
The old saying that we are to "use things and
love people" especially applies to kindred spirit
friendships. A relationship pursued by deception is never God's way. Instead, Paul admonishes that our love for one another should
spring from "a pure heart and a good conscience" (1 Timothy 1:5). It's pretty hard to
practice that kind of love when lies and secret
motives draw you together.

Manipulation clouds the beauty of true
friendship. It does so because it is rooted in
selfish, not selfless love. Deception violates
boundaries of propriety with its "She won't do

what I want, so I must trick her into a place of compliance" mentality. As a pastor's wife, I've heard women threaten to leave the church if I wouldn't be the perfect friend to them. Don't mistake manipulation for friendship.

One gray spring day, Shannon moved her ragged family of three into Tony and Cassie's basement. Shannon and Cassie had been friends for years. So when Shannon fell on hard times and found herself homeless, Cassie generously offered to share their home. If she had known Shannon's bent toward manipulation, Cassie would never have opened the door.

"I was pretty naive," Cassie said later. "We were friends. I guess I just didn't want to admit she was using me."

But using their friendship was exactly what Shannon proceeded to do. While Cassie was away at work, Shannon spent more and more time with Tony, Cassie's husband. She flattered him. She did the things for him that Cassie didn't have the time to do. Ultimately, Shannon launched an affair undermining Tony and Cassie's marriage. Cassie's friendship, it seemed, had been a convenient channel to someone else.

The story doesn't end there. Tony, certain he had rediscovered true love, made plans to divorce his wife and marry Shannon. However, he soon discovered that Shannon was using him as well.

One evening before they were married, Tony and Shannon argued violently. Shannon left in a huff, swearing she would never be back. A day later, a repentant Tony went searching for Shannon, only to find her already involved with another man. She hadn't really loved him at all. Tony was simply a channel to her real goal—a house for her and her children.

Shannon's goals were admirable enough. Marriage and owning a home are worthy aspirations. Shannon's wrong came when she began using her friends and violating their trust to achieve her goals. When we need something from friends, we should ask, not deceive them into helping. If they refuse, our friendship should equally respect their honesty and limitations. When we have to manipulate people to reach our goals, we've stepped outside God's plan for friendship.

More often, however, emotional levers are used to manipulate friendships. Some friends appear generous but have actually attached an invisible string of obligation to every gift. While guilt and obligation are powerful emotional ties, they destroy intimacy. Instead of allowing a healthy, honest give-and-take, manipulation forces a response. The response becomes void of any emotional meaning and ultimately may fail completely. Gifts aren't wrong in a friendship, but they should always be offered freely.

Fear is another manipulator. It simply isn't fair to force a relationship by wielding threats.

Someone once told me of her husband's tendency to do this. When they argued, he would bring up painful childhood memories she had told him and use them to wound her all over again. Obviously, she was afraid to create waves in their relationship. It should have been equally obvious to him that their friendship was on the way out the door.

Trust, not fear, is the bedrock for any intimate relationship. This is why First John 4:18 says, "There is no fear in love. But perfect love drives out fear, because fear has to do with punishment." Outwardly intimidation may look like intimacy, but it will never feel that way. It is impossible for fear and love to co-exist.

Warning #3: The Smothering Embrace of Possessiveness

Did you ever as a child pledge to be a playmate's best friend? I recalled the social struggles of my elementary years as I watched my daughter negotiate the possessive alliances between herself and her friends. To be one neighbor girl's friend usually entailed a promise not to play with a rival and vice versa. Usually we outgrow such possessiveness. As we mature, we realize that friends are capable of loyalty to more than one person. We realize also that trying to capture a friendship ultimately crushes the life out of it.

Isolation, jealousy and frustration are warning signs that a friendship is becoming posses-

sive. Jealousy is that selfish attitude that be-
grudges someone else time with a friend. Frustration is jealousy's twin sister. If plans with a
friend are blocked by another is it frustration or
simply disappointment that you feel?

Disappointment is frustration that has been
relinquished. While we might wish things had
gone differently and are disappointed, we are
willing to let go and move on. When we experience jealousy or frustration in a relationship, it
should be an indication that we have taken the
control of our lives away from God. Rather
than looking to God to work things out, we've
forged adamantly ahead with our own desires
only to find our way blocked. If we persist in
our frustration, it will eventually turn into depression or a possessiveness that will smother
the friendship we prize.

Possessiveness is also seen in a friendship
that gravitates toward isolation. It is important
to realize that isolation is not the same as privacy. Obviously, we all need a certain measure
of privacy in a relationship for intimacy to
grow. The memories of solitary walks with
friends or moments spent together in prayer
are cherished experiences. Unhealthy isolation
is when we purposely close out the world to
create the illusion of intimacy. Relationships
that isolate us from others are doomed to fail.
Instead, there should be a refreshing openness
to sharing times with others as well as enjoying
time alone. When we find we always need to

be alone, it's time to question whether the level of relationship is appropriate.

Warning #4: Foundational Spiritual Differences

What about friendships with non-Christians? Perhaps you have recently become a Christian. Now you wonder if you can hold onto your old friendships while embracing your new life in Christ. Let me reassure you that becoming a Christian does not mean that you can't have non-Christian friends. Jesus Himself was called the "friend of sinners" (Matthew 11:19). It does mean, however, that conversation and activities we share with friends should be honoring to Jesus Christ. In this light, friendships are possible with non-Christians, but intimate friendships are ill advised (see 2 Corinthians 6:14).

We become like those we spend time with. Proverbs 13:20 warns: "He who walks with the wise grows wise, but a companion of fools suffers harm." The word "fools" in this verse means those who pursue ungodliness. The challenge here is to choose friends carefully. Friends who are not interested in the things of Christ or tempt us to turn away from Him are friends we can do without.

Looking back on my difficult friendship with Sue, I can see many of these warning signs in operation. There was a dark possessiveness about her friendship. She wanted me to visit at her home every week with no exceptions. Even my well intentioned phone calls were not acceptable substitutes. She wasn't interested in joining me for any of the events at church, although I invited her repeatedly. In addition, her continual negativity acted like acid on my own Christian perspective. When I risked trying to work out the difficulties, she ceremoniously hung up on me and quit attending church. Later it filtered back to me that Sue and her family quit attending our church because I hadn't been a good enough friend to her. Clearly she thought she could manipulate me through a massive guilt trip.

Maybe you've been through a similar experience. I'm not suggesting that we be overly introspective about our friendships. But when you sense that things are going astray, check for signs of compromise, manipulation or possessiveness. Your friendship may not be headed in the right direction.

Kindred Spirits Gone Astray

The best safeguard to kindred spirit friendships is to keep Christ as your focus. In fact, Christ's right to direct our lives as Christians cannot be stressed enough. His authority extends not only over ethical issues, lifestyles and questions of guidance; but also over friendships as well. Holiness is the Christian life—not just an aspect of it. It doesn't work to live for Christ on Sunday but disregard

Him on Saturday night. Jesus noted that we are incapable of worshiping two things simultaneously. As he observed: "Either [we] will hate the one and love the other, or [we] will be devoted to the one and despise the other" (Matthew 6:24). The principles of lordship are clear: God will not share control of our lives, and we serve the thing we worship. Even something as rewarding as a kindred spirit friendship can enslave us if God is not kept central in that relationship.

Homosexuality exemplifies an intimate friendship that often starts out as an emotional need but deteriorates into physical depravity. Our society's tendency to equate intimacy with sexuality is also wrong because friendship can be intimate without a hint of sexual misconduct. However, the Bible warns us that if we reject Christ's lordship over our lives, our relationships can become skewed.

> The wrath of God is being revealed from heaven against all the godlessness and wickedness of men who suppress the truth by their wickedness, since what may be known about God is plain to them, because God has made it plain to them. For since the creation of the world God's invisible qualities—his eternal power and divine nature—have been clearly seen, being understood from what has been made, so that men are without excuse.

For although they knew God, they neither glorified him as God nor gave thanks
to him, but their thinking became futile
and their foolish hearts were darkened.
Although they claimed to be wise, they
became fools and exchanged the glory of
the immortal God for images made to
look like mortal men and birds and animals and reptiles.

Therefore God gave them over in the sinful desires of their hearts to sexual impu-
rity for the degrading of their bodies with
one another. (Romans 1:18-25)

Here's how it happens. Cutting ourselves off
from God, we quickly lose our sense of moral
direction. Confusion clouds our thinking. Instead of being led by God's principles, we are
left to the whims of emotions that are no longer
under His control. Doing what "feels right"
only leads deeper into depravity. While we
tend to think of the sexual aspects of homosexuality, it is really the emotional addiction
that prepares the way for physical involvement. Few people start out seeking a homosexual relationship. Instead they are seeking to be
loved.

Focus on the Family once ran an article on homosexuality. The article was essentially three
testimonies of former gays: two lesbians and
one homosexual. They shared how they became caught up in homosexuality and how

faith in Christ enabled them to leave that life-style. The testimonies of both former lesbians highlight the danger of emotionally addictive friendships. One wrote of her initial experience with a college roommate:

> Neither of us dated men much, and she always felt upset because no one loved her. I was struggling with the same feelings. My roommate and I started spending a lot of time together. It wasn't long before we began relating to each other on a deep emotional level. I didn't set out to find a woman to love; I set out to find someone to love me.

> The moment I crossed over the line into homosexuality was right out of "Movie of the Week." We were sitting in our room late at night, and it got very quiet. She extended her hand, and I took it. We hugged, and then we looked into each other's eyes. She kissed me, and then we became intimate. . . . Although there was a physical attraction, lesbianism was an emotional attachment for me. (*Focus on the Family*, March 1994, 2-3)

Later in the article, the other former lesbian further confirmed this confusion about homosexuality when she identified emotional co-dependency—not physical attraction—as being the root of nearly all gay relationships.

Co-dependency is simply trying to draw our identity from someone else. The co-dependent is keenly aware of a great hole in her soul that she is unable to fill. It is a nearly universal feeling that is more intense for some. It's been called a God-shaped vacuum. In that sense, we are all co-dependent. While God would like us to be dependent on Him, we usually try to fill that vacuum with other substitutes. Homosexuality is one substitute. The relational high of closeness—the feeling of being loved and understood—draws some friends into an emotional addiction. The step to physical involvement may be only a matter of time. The more such behavior is reinforced, the more "natural" it seems. What began as a conscious choice has become a powerful, binding addiction. In essence, lesbians become prisoners of their own depravity (see Romans 1:28).

This is not a positive alternative form of friendship as so many would have us believe. Romans 1:29–31 notes that those who actively reject God "become filled with every kind of wickedness, evil, greed and depravity. They are full of envy, murder, strife, deceit and malice. They are gossips, slanderers, God-haters, insolent, arrogant and boastful; they invent ways of doing evil; they disobey their parents; they are senseless, faithless, heartless, ruthless." Certainly not every homosexual or lesbian manifests all the qualities above. It is clear, however, that this lifestyle is characterized by depravity and the truckload of heartache that goes with it.

Warning #5: *Emotional Enmeshment*

While most women won't end up in lesbian relationships, many will allow themselves to become emotionally dependent on their friends. Take Laura's and Michelle's friendship, for example.

Both Laura and Michelle were married and had satisfactory sexual relationships with their husbands. Unfortunately, neither woman had a growing friendship with her husband. As Laura described it, "He lives in his world. The kids and I live in mine. I don't like it, but that's just the way it's always been."

Their joint loneliness was one thing that drew Laura and Michelle to one another. But difficulties at home were only one of many interests the two women shared. In many ways, their friendship had the makings of a kindred spirit relationship. Eventually, their times together included the sharing of deep confidences.

There is nothing wrong with their friendship as described so far. Yet slowly a key change began to take place. Increasingly, time was devoted to this relationship alone. Less and less time was spent nurturing their failing marriages. Virtually no time was spent developing other friendships. Eventually, the two women became almost inseparable—not only in their activities, but in their emotional responses as well. When Laura was up, Michelle was up. When one was discouraged, the other was overwhelmed with concern. Somewhere along the way, the lines that define individual identity were becoming blurred.

When Laura's husband accepted a job transfer that moved them out of town, the parting uncovered a deep emotional addiction that left both women trying to pick up the pieces of their shattered worlds. Although there was never a physical relationship between them, Michelle and Laura had allowed their friendship to replace Christ as Lord of their lives.

In contrast, a friendship focused on Christ enables friends to maintain separate identities that can enrich each other. One author describes the balance this way:

> When we feel our emotional boundaries, we can discriminate between our feelings and another's feelings. We can hear another's feelings and not have to fix them. We can discern what issues are ours and what issues belong to the other person. (Katherine 1991, 113)

For example, while goodbyes may still be painful, it is possible to affirm that this special friend was only part of your life, not life itself. It is not wrong to love a friend deeply, but if you find yourself thinking, "I really couldn't cope without her," then you've probably crossed the line from friendship to addiction. We should draw our life and identity from Christ, not one another.

Now consider another friendship. Chris had known Kathy for years. As a third grader, Chris spent Wednesday evenings in a kid's club where Kathy was a leader. One evening, Kathy explained how a person could receive Christ and gave the opportunity for the children to do so. Chris realized this was a decision she wanted to make. The following day, in a simple prayer, she welcomed Christ into her life. It was a decision that not only changed Chris' life, but one that left a warm spot in her heart for this older woman as well.

Third grade came and went. In high school, Chris became a cheerleader along with Kathy's daughter, Karen. The joint activity brought the girls to Kathy's home regularly, where Chris again found herself warmed by Kathy's tenderness.

So when Chris was facing some personal difficulties in college, she turned to Kathy and received far more than her counsel. As a joint commitment, the two women began meeting weekly for prayer, Bible study, Scripture memorization and sharing. With Christ at the center of their relationship, God used the friendship that blossomed through those times to transform both women. For Chris, Kathy became the model of a Christian woman, mother and wife she so desperately needed to see. For Kathy, Chris' friendship provided an outlet for her God-given gift of encouragement.

Today, the original needs that brought them together have long since ceased, and they no longer meet regularly. Yet both women are available to minister to one another as God would have them. While each has a separate identity, they are deeply joined through the ongoing love of Christ. In fact, Chris illustrated the purpose of kindred spirit friendships when she said: "Kathy is the one person who has influenced my life more than anyone else, because she has modeled for me how to walk with Christ."

God wants us to experience the richness of kindred spirit relationships. Outside of a relationship with Him, none is sweeter or more powerful. However, if your kindred friendship has taken a path similar to Laura's and Michelle's, you may need some professional help to get your friendship back on track. Emotional addictions are learned over time. Through God's strength and wisdom, you can change your friendship into something more satisfying.

Recognizing the warning signs of a friendship going sour is just the first step. It may not be necessary to abandon the friendship. How God would have us work through problems with a friend to strengthen or save a relationship is the subject of the next chapter.

Making It Yours

1. Read Romans 14:13-21. What do you think Paul meant when he wrote: "Make up your mind not to put any stumbling block or obstacle in your brother's way"? How can urging a friend to compromise on her convictions become a stumbling block?

2. In Jesus' day the Pharisees used a system of binding and non-binding oaths. A binding oath was a promise you intended to keep, while a non-binding oath was something like the childhood practice of making a promise while crossing your fingers behind your back. Jesus confronted such practices with strong language. Read Matthew 5:33-37. Have you ever had someone use a promise to manipulate you? What happened, and how did you feel toward that person afterward?

3. Read the passages below. What biblical guidelines can you use to help you treat your relationships more honestly?

   Matthew 5:37.
   Ephesians 4:25.
   James 4:13-17.

4. Instead of manipulating a relationship through deception or intimidation, what is the biblical model for relationships? (2 Thessalonians 2:3-8; 2 Timothy 2:24,25)

5. Read Galatians 5:19-26. What does jealousy reveal about the nature of your friendship? How can God enable us to change the character of our friendships? (see 5:24-25)

6. Second Corinthians 6:14 says: "Do not be yoked together with unbelievers." Does this principle apply only to marriage, or to intimate friendships as well? (see Psalm   1:1-4; 2 Corinthians 6:14-18)

7. Read Romans 1:18-32. Do you think co-dependent friendships are just as wrong as homosexual relationships? How are they similar? In what ways are they different?

8. If you are entangled in a co-dependent friendship, seek Christian counseling. Co-dependency is rooted in underlying causes. Diffusing co-dependent patterns usually requires a competent counselor who can help you understand those causes, deal with them and learn how to have healthy intimate friendships.

If your friendships have become homosexual, the following agencies are specifically equipped to help.

Exodus International   (415) 454-1017
P.O. 2121
San Rafael, CA 94912

Desert Stream   (310) 572-0140
12488 Venice Blvd.
Los Angeles, CA 90066-3804

His Heart Ministries   (303) 369-2961
P.O. Box 12321
Aurora, CO 80011

Metanoia Ministries   (206) 783-3500
P.O. Box 33039
Seattle, WA 98103

Chapter 7

Walls, Bridges or Gates?

On Sunday, August 13, 1961, the identity of the city of Berlin changed from being the largest city in Germany to the city divided by the infamous Berlin Wall. For the next 28 years, the Wall encircled West Berlin like a giant convoluted concrete scar. As a boundary, the Berlin Wall defined East Germany from West Germany. While one side was committed to communism, the other side pursued democracy and free enterprise. In time, the Wall effectively separated and protected two identities within the German people until its removal in 1989.

People establish boundaries in their relationships, too. Unlike the Berlin Wall, we need to develop clear, but loving, limitations. We need to be able to convey the message that says, "I'm involved in this friendship to this point, but no further." When personal limitations are unclear in relationships, confusion and hurt are inevitable.

How are loving boundaries built? Is confrontation necessary? Should we roll out our rights like Berlin's wall of concrete and barbed wire, daring our boldest friends to trespass? How does God desire that Christians deal with tension in relationships that have gone sour?

Pick Your Battles

Life is full of differences—some major, some minor. Discerning the difference between major and minor conflicts is a big part of conflict resolution. To know the difference, we need to think about our values and ask: What are the key issues in this conflict and how will these issues threaten my values?

Here are examples of my values, some of which are unique to marriage and others common to all friendships:

Mutual trust and respect among my
children and spouse
Personal faith in God
Responsible behavior in my children
Right to personal interests and feelings
Opportunity to learn or to fail without
retribution

Everyone's list is unique and evolves as life moves along. The values on your list can help you pick what is worth differing over. This perspective will save you from battling an exhaustive haze of smaller conflicts. Maturity is partly knowing which conflicts are worth the time, risk and energy.

Like a pilot flying a plane within a bank of clouds, life's course can often seem direction-less. Left to visual cues, we'd be lost in no time. Only as the pilot looks to his instruments is he able to stay on course. Likewise, instead of fac-ing every conflict as a personal assignment, we need to ask God for discernment. He is always prepared to give us the direction we need if we are open to His guidance.

Love Gift

One way of resolving conflict is to relinquish the fight before it starts. Someone has called this approach to conflict a "love gift." A love gift is when you surrender your right to be right. In effect you decide that the relationship is more important than the issue at hand.

One spring afternoon my husband had gone out of town to a conference. I would be on my own for the week to come, yet I was deter-mined to have a positive week with the kids. My optimism was short lived. Crash! The sound of breaking glass emanated from the rear of the house setting my nerves jangling. Rushing toward the family room, I discovered four-year-old Michael standing with a plastic bat in hand crying uncontrollably. "I'm sorry. I'm sorry. I'm sorry."

A quick look explained the story. He had been playing with a golf ball, bouncing it off his resilient plastic bat. Obviously the odds were against him. It wasn't long before the ball took one mighty bounce and went right through the window. He sobbed out his confession, hot tears coursing over his cheeks.

Now I could have responded to Michael in anger. It was beginning to rain and I had a group of ladies scheduled to meet in this room the very next morning. All of these were good reasons for me to be very upset about having to deal with a shattered window. In addition, Michael had been disobedient by doing something he had been told not to do. In fact, I believe my words were: "I don't want you playing with Dad's golf balls, because it would be too easy for one to go through a window." Nearly prophetic, huh? But instead of confronting Michael, I gave him a love gift.

Getting down on my knees, I gathered his shaking, sniffling body in my arms and said, "That's OK. I know you didn't mean to do it. I'm not angry. It was an accident." It was one of my more noble motherly moments, believe me. Not only was Michael surprised and relieved; but I was a bit surprised at myself. The effect however, was beautiful. A potentially destructive conflict was set aside, while an important relationship was nourished.

Granted, it is much easier to offer love gifts to red-eyed, sniffling preschoolers than adult friends who should know better and aren't as quick to own up to their wrongs. But God offers love gifts to us all the time. If God disciplined us for every personal sin, we would always be sitting in the proverbial corner for life. Instead, God asks us to confess the sins we are aware of, but He graciously promises to "purify us from ALL unrighteousness" (1 John 1:9, emphasis added). That total cleansing is God's love gift.

Proverbs 19:11 says: "A man's wisdom gives him patience; it is to his glory to overlook an offense." This verse doesn't say that the offender will acknowledge your gift. It does promise that a lifestyle marked by grace is one that radiates God's glory. So look again at the conflict at hand. Is it all that imperative that you resolve it, or can you simply offer a love gift?

Preventive Confrontation

Although we do not like it, confrontation probably offers the greatest opportunity to make or break a friendship. One evening, Linda shared with me how she learned this through her friendship with Angela.

Linda had moved away from home to pursue graduate studies at the University of Washington. It was there that she met Angela. Angela was also working on her degree in elementary education. The two women quickly became acquainted through the classes they shared and often studied together. They also were both Christians. That was where their similarities ended.

Linda came from a Christian upbringing in a middle-class home in Portland, Oregon. Angela's background was a large family in a tiny, rural town in Mississippi. The cultural differences presented obstacles between the two women. For example, Angela would often phone in the evenings just to visit, yet to Linda the lengthy conversations often seemed superficial. She soon began to find excuses to cut their talks short. If Angela hadn't questioned the increasing tension between them, their friendship might have drifted apart before it ever really began. But when Angela asked Linda what was bothering her, a conversation ensued that resulted in new insights for both of them.

It was hard for Linda to answer Angela's question by telling her that she didn't want to spend time talking on the phone about superficial things, but she did. In turn, Angela told her that this was the way that people initiated friendships where she was raised. As their understanding of each other grew, they could better accommodate each other's needs and preferences. Other differences continued to arise as their friendship progressed. Painful as such talks often were, Angela and Linda talked through each one.

"We really had to learn how to work out differences—to talk about them," Linda said. "Even though the differences weren't always resolved, we learned to pray for our friendship and for each other, and that would ease the tension."

Talk about the Little Things

Linda and Angela's friendship highlights two important aspects to preventive confrontation. First, the goal should be to preserve the relationship. Their goal was never to conquer the other in an argument. Instead, understanding and renewed commitment was the focus. One way they did that was to talk about irritations before they became open wounds. In her book, *The Dance of Intimacy*, Harriet Goldhor Lerner writes:

> Intimacy means that we can be who we are in a relationship, and allow the other person to do the same. Being who we are requires that we can talk openly about things that are important to us, that we take a clear position on where we stand on important emotional issues, and that we clarify the limits of what is acceptable and tolerable to us in a relationship. Allowing the other person to do the same means that we can stay emotionally connected to that other party who thinks, feels, and believes differently, without needing to change, convince, or fix the other. (Lerner 1989, 3)

This describes Linda and Angela's attitude. Instead of letting conflicts push them apart, they were using their differences to create intimacy.

Most friends wait too long to confront their differences. The first offense is passed off as a onetime occurrence. "Surely it will never happen again." Then it happens again. Little by little the offenses add up. Emotional temperatures rise until we can contain our irritation no longer. Then comes the day of an explosive confrontation or a retreat to pursue friendships elsewhere. How much better if we would seek to understand differences earlier. Proverbs 27:5-6 says:

> Better is open rebuke
>> than hidden love.
> Wounds from a friend can be trusted,
>> but an enemy multiplies kisses.

How about it? Do you wait too long to confront a friend? An unresolved conflict is like having a pebble in your shoe. It might not bother you at the outset, but hike a mile or so and you'll limp in pain. Instead, ask God to help you settle your differences early, before wounding occurs.

Prayer—God's Super Glue

The second thing Linda and Angela did right was to make Christ the focus of their friendship. From the start, prayer was an important part of their time together. Linda recalls: "Very early during our time together, Angela asked me to be her prayer partner. This really surprised me. I didn't feel that we were that compatible to be prayer partners. Yet it was prayer that brought us together. Despite all these other things, the oneness we shared in Christ allowed our relationship with each other to grow."

When conflicts arose, Linda and Angela continued to pray. They prayed for their friendship, and they prayed for one another. By faith they practiced their unity in Christ.

Prayer changes our heart because it is rooted in personal forgiveness. Jesus gave H is disciples a model for prayer in what today is referred to as "The Lord's Prayer" (Matthew 6:9-13). In it not only is God praised and exalted as Lord, but we are also guided to seek unity with our fellow man. Jesus said we are to pray: "Forgive us our debts, as we also have forgiven our debtors" (6:12). You see, it is impossible to pray effectively with a heart full of bitterness. God turns a deaf ear to such prayers. Yet He delights to answer the one seeking forgiveness and resolution.

Close friendships aren't maintained by some irresistible magnetic energy. As one author observed, "Intimacy is not about the initial Velcro stage of relationships" (Lerner 1989, 1). Rather, intimacy has to do with how well we can balance being separate and being connected. Prayer, like some kind of spiritual super glue, negotiates this paradox. We come to Christ in prayer individually with the result that our hearts are bonded together in Him. We are separate, but we are also deeply connected. Prayer is the foundation for intimate Christian friendship.

How do we handle conflicts that get out of control? Often they are not easy to talk about. And what about a friendship where praying with the offending person seems out of the question? What is the biblical approach to confronting a friendship gone bad?

Confronting a Friendship Gone Bad

The stories of David and King Saul give seven steps for effective confrontation. Initially, King Saul was impressed by David and had arranged for the courageous youth to work in the palace after David's victory over Goliath. But Saul was a troubled man. He was extremely paranoid. Any praise David received for his prowess in battle made Saul insanely jealous. Sometimes, Saul would rage for seemingly no reason at all. Then he would call for David to come play his harp. Somehow the music seemed to calm Saul's tortured mind.

Certainly there must have been close ties between the two men. Even Saul's son, Jonathan, was David's closest friend. It must have been hard for David as he watched his initial friendship with King Saul grow increasingly estranged.

David was patient. He was forgiving. But as the years passed, Saul's paranoia turned to obsession. Ultimately Saul became convinced that David wanted to usurp the throne.

Fleeing for his life, David retreated to the wilderness with a ragged band of outcasts. Yet, even there, Saul relentlessly pursued him. It was no surprise then, that when David was in a position to ambush Saul, his men encouraged him to take revenge. Instead, David showed his men how to handle a friendship gone bad. It happened like this.

Saul had received word that David was camped at a certain place in the wilderness. Immediately Saul was in pursuit. Sensing him hot on his trail, David and his men hid in a large cave. In a comical turn of events, Saul stopped near the cave and went in to relieve himself. Looking on from the shadows, David's men whispered, "This is the day the LORD spoke of when he said to you, 'I will give your enemy into your hands for you to deal with as you wish' " (1 Samuel 24:4).

1. Await God's Timing

For countless months, and finally years, David had run from King Saul. David was innocent, but there seemed no way to defend himself from Saul's accusations and deadly intentions. Now the opportunity for revenge—the moment for confrontation—was at hand. It was finally time to act.

Timing is critical to confrontation. When it comes to resolving differences, people basically fall into one of two groups. There are the *fight-ers*—those that want to wade in and settle the problem right away. Then there are the *flighters*—those who retreat and would just as soon not talk about the situation at all. Obviously, knowing the right time to confront can make or break the ensuing negotiations.

So how does a person recognize the right time? The first step is to pray and ask God to show you. I've done this many times, not only with conflicts but also when seeking guidance for the right time to witness to a friend. God has never failed to answer.

One day as I agonized over a painful conversation that had to take place, I prayed: "God, if You want me to talk with this person, then have him contact me." I wasn't surprised when the phone rang later that day and I heard the words, "I was just wondering if I've done something to offend you?" God is more than willing to help us make peace.

Another factor that made this a right moment for David was the mutual vulnerability the situation offered. We tend to be territorial creatures with places where we feel more secure. Sometimes trying to settle an issue works best when both individuals step into a neutral setting. I know a pastor who said that he and his wife often talk over their differences in a restaurant where raising their voices is out of the question. It saves them from saying things they would later regret.

For David and Saul the desert gave them neutral ground. For the moment they were both equally vulnerable.

The opportunity to talk is another key factor in determining such a time. Don't try to hurriedly settle differences in the church hallway on Sunday morning. Find a time when you can talk uninterrupted and face-to-face if possible. Passing off a mumbled apology in an inappropriate setting can sound insincere and make a wound deeper still.

2. Resist the Urge for Revenge

Looking back at First Samuel 24, we see David's heart momentarily swayed by temptation. Silently he crept toward his enemy. Rather than strike a deadly blow, however, David only cut off the corner of Saul's robe. Yet even that slight act of revenge grieved his heart. Saul was God's appointed king. Who was David to take revenge into his own hands?

Revenge is a natural instinct to strike back when we've been wounded. As one man said, "Life being what it is, one dreams of revenge" (Byrne 1986, 274). Yet as David realized, revenge is God's place, not ours, even in the smallest measure. In God's hands revenge becomes justice. In our hands, revenge only further embitters a rocky relationship.

One summer I was working as the stock clerk in a small department store. I enjoyed my job and the people I worked with. I enjoyed them all, except Della. Della was in charge of the linens department and she ruled over her realm of sheets and towels with a mighty hand. What's more, Della loved to tell everyone else what needed to be done, when and how. She was a self-made tyrant and I was not excused from her lectures. Over time my irritation burned into red-hot coals of anger. I determined somehow I'd take revenge. Then came the day that an immense shipment of sheets came in. Back in the warehouse I checked them in and priced several cases. Right before lunch, I rolled the small mountain of linens to her department. Leaving them in a main aisle, I went off to lunch. I can still remember her screeching about having to spend all day getting those sheets put away.

Della had a new, wary respect for me from that day on. Certainly my fellow employees applauded my deed. I had finally gotten the best of Della. Not many were sympathetic as she worked through lunch to organize her disorderly department. But what about my relationship with Della? It hadn't been off to a great start, but it was certainly finished now. We worked together when we had to and spoke only when necessary. Any chance for a friendship was buried when I took revenge.

3. Treat the Other with Respect

So David resisted taking full revenge and repented of the small revenge he had taken.

Then as Saul left the cave, David courageously stepped forward to settle the breach between them. "My lord the king!" David shouted. Then he "bowed down and prostrated himself with his face to the ground" (1 Samuel 24:8). Saul was David's bitter enemy. Yet even as he confronted this difficult relationship, David still treated Saul with the utmost respect.

Respecting others is difficult enough on our good days, let alone when we are angry. But respect sets the stage for what follows (see Proverbs 18:21). If we treat another with respect, we may enjoy the sweetness of reconciliation.

4. Seek to Clarify Misunderstandings

Only after David had gained Saul's attention through right timing and respect did David help Saul put their conflict into perspective. He said,

> Why do you listen when men say, "David is bent on harming you"? This day you have seen with your own eyes how the LORD delivered you into my hands in the cave. Some urged me to kill you, but I spared you; I said, "I will not lift my hand against my master, because he is the LORD's anointed." See, my father, look at this piece of your robe in my hand! I cut off the corner of your robe but did not kill you. (24:9-11)

While our unity in Christ is true, it is also hard kept in daily life. Every person has their own perspective. Misunderstandings are inevitable. When they happen, a friend bent on resolution will listen carefully and help put things in perspective. This is what David was doing. He was trying to clarify the misunderstanding between himself and Saul.

5. Receive Apologies with Grace

Saul was nearly speechless when David finished speaking.

"Is that your voice, David my son?" Saul called out. "You are more righteous than I" (24:16-17). Then Saul broke down and started to cry.

How we long to hear the words, "I'm sorry" or "you were right" when we've been hurt. Isn't it ironic that when such apologies finally come, we often don't want to accept them? Instead we often cling to our rags of self-righteous indignation. After all, accepting another's apology means canceling the pity party we had underway. Instead, Jesus calls us to a lifestyle characterized by His grace.

The apostle Peter asked, "Lord, how many times shall I forgive my brother when he sins against me?" (Matthew 18:21). Jesus answered Peter with a parable in which a rich man forgives another man an enormous debt. Later this forgiven man fails to offer similar forgiveness to someone else. When the news reaches the rich man, he has the original debtor arrested and severely disciplined. "Shouldn't you have had mercy on your fellow servant just as I had on you?" the rich man asked (18:33).

The answer is obvious, isn't it? Jesus concluded His parable with a warning: "This is how my heavenly Father will treat each of you unless you forgive your brother from your heart" (18:35). If we've been forgiven so much, how dare we refuse to accept the apology of another?

6. Reaffirm Your Love

Saul ends his conversation begging for assurance that he'd been forgiven by David, "Swear to me by the LORD," Saul begged, "that you will not cut off my descendants or wipe out my name from my father's family" (1 Samuel 24:21). It was traditional that when someone usurped the throne, they killed off all the relatives of the former royal line. This assured the new king of fewer challengers. Saul knew David would one day ascend to the throne of Israel and wanted a promise that when that day came, David would not kill his descendants. I believe David confirmed the vow to demonstrate his forgiveness.

We all need such reassurance when we admit our wrong. Our fear of rejection is just below the surface. We wonder, "Will they bring this up again? Am I really forgiven?" This is why Proverbs 17:9 advises:

He who covers over an offense promotes
   love,
   but whoever repeats the matter
   separates close friends.

Our actions speak louder than our words.

In her book, *What Happens When Women Pray,*
Evelyn Christenson told a beautiful story of
reconciliation. One summer afternoon, Evelyn
called a woman in her church to pass along an
answer to prayer. Unfortunately, the woman
on the other end responded with words that
deeply offended her. Later as Evelyn prayed
about the matter, God led her to Second Corinthians 2:5-8:

> If anyone has caused grief . . . The punish-
> ment inflicted on him by the majority is
> sufficient for him. Now instead, you
> ought to forgive and comfort him, so that
> he will not be overwhelmed by excessive
> sorrow. I urge you, therefore, to reaffirm
> your love for him.

Evelyn had certainly been grieved by this
woman. Now God spelled out the answer to
the rift between them. First, she was to forgive.
Second, she was to reaffirm her love for the offender.

The next question was how to do this. Evelyn
shares God's answer:

> On the first Sunday morning we were
> back in church, I spied her sitting on the

opposite side of the sanctuary . . . I didn't hear one word the pastor said as I kept praying, "Lord, if You want me to confirm this love, You have to put her where I'm going to run into her. I'm not going to make a fool of myself. . . . And so help me!" At the close of the service I opened the big double doors at the back of the sanctuary and almost knocked her down! There she was! And what did I have to do? I put my arms around her and said only one thing, "I just want you to know I love you." And the tears started to roll. (Christenson 1975, 125-128)

The apostle Paul urged us, "Make every effort to keep the unity of the Spirit through the bond of peace" (Ephesians 4:3). Have differences brought you and your friend to a place of confrontation? Ask God for the strength to forgive. Then ask Him to show you how to reaffirm that sister or brother who's hurting. Make every effort to mend the rift. Don't be tempted to stop short with a superficial, "I forgive you." Highlight your words with a gentle touch, a smile or a brief note. Reaffirm your love for your humbled friend.

But what about the friendship gone sour that won't respond to loving confrontation? It takes two to resolve a conflict. Sometimes, despite all your prayers, sensitivity and efforts, you still get the feeling that you are the victim—or soon will be. Does Christian forgiveness require us to be doormats allowing others to walk all over us?

7. *Establish Boundaries*

Did David return to the palace with Saul after their talk? Take a look at the final verse of First Samuel 24: "Then Saul returned home, but David and his men went up to the stronghold." David didn't trust Saul and with good reason. Saul had been repentant before but later changed his mind and renewed his attacks on David. Common sense told David that even though he accepted Saul's apology, he still needed to keep his distance, at least until Saul's actions confirmed his words. It was a wise decision, for only two chapters later Saul was again pursuing David.

In situations like these, Christian friendship helps both parties by setting boundaries that the offender seems unable to set. Don't be misled. God does not condone abusive relationships!

First, think about the limits you need to set. David needed physical protection. He chose to live away from Saul's courts, despite Saul's show of remorse. In effect, David was saying, "I'm not coming back until you've demonstrated that you've changed, and that we can live safely side by side." The physical distance between them was David's boundary.

Second, setting up boundaries means defining a clear bottom line position: "If you begin to do or say this, then I am going to respond by doing this." A lack of boundaries in a relationship leaves the victim with only a few choices.

Walls, Bridges or Gates?

Relational walls are easy to build. Unlike the Berlin Wall, relational walls can go up in the blink of an eye and remain in place for a lifetime. Sometimes, cutting off a difficult friendship is emotionally safe. Yet ironically, intimacy requires working through difficulties with another. Just as hot embers temper the steel of the mightiest sword, so negotiating differences strengthens relationships. Proverbs 27:17 says: "As iron sharpens iron, so one man sharpens another." Conflict might be painful, but it is not necessarily bad. Walls provide safety, but always at the cost of intimacy.

Relational bridges, on the other hand, connect people. They are built to span what would otherwise be unnegotiable. They allow for an unrestrained flow of ideas. But when too much traffic flows one way or another on a bridge, progress can come to a standstill. It's at times like this that we need to regulate the relational "traffic" problems we are facing.

Gates are the only healthy way to regulate a relationship out of control. This doesn't guarantee you will be able to continue your friendship at the depth you once did. For a variety of reasons, you may sense or desire a loss of closeness. What gates do is protect both friends at neither one's expense.

Which choice is the right one for you in your friendship? That's an answer only God can give you. It would be too simplistic to prescribe one solution as a cure-all. Walls, bridges or gates—there is undoubtedly a time and place for each approach. May God help us choose wisely.

Making It Yours

1. Personalize the "Pick Your Battles" segment of this chapter by listing your values. How will this help you when conflicts arise?

2. How does preventive confrontation differ from confronting in a friendship gone bad? (You might find it helpful to refer to Chapter 6: When It Isn't Working)

3. As a review, list the steps for confronting a friendship gone bad. Behind each step, write the supportive verses from First Samuel 24.

   A.
   B.
   C.
   D.
   E.
   F.
   G.

4. How does setting boundaries in a relationship demonstrate Christian love?

5. Read Jeremiah 12:14-17. How did God set boundaries in his relationship with Israel?

6. Agree/Disagree: "God does not condone abusive relationships."

7. How does the title "Walls, Bridges or Gates?" describe three ways we react to others? Take a moment to think and pray about your friendships. Is God directing you to make some changes?

Chapter 8

The Truth about Risk

Ephesus was a bustling port on the banks of the sparkling Mediterranean Sea. God was blessing the apostle Paul's ministry in Ephesus, and a young church was taking shape. But it was the friends he'd left behind in Corinth that cast a shadow over his thoughts.

Some years earlier, Paul had established a church in Corinth. Soon after Paul left, however, the church began to compromise their Christian stand. Pagan lifestyles were embraced by the congregation. One man was even living openly in an incestuous relationship with his mother! (See 1 Corinthians 5:1). In addition, they began to compare Paul's ministry with other local preachers. Even Paul's own credentials were under attack.

Hoping to set things right, Paul responded quickly from Ephesus with several frank letters. The result wasn't encouraging. Some at Corinth misunderstood Paul's intentions. They felt wounded by Paul's rebuke. The friendships that existed between Paul and these young Christians threatened to end in an emotional schism. No doubt Paul's heart ached as he sat down to write:

> Make room for us in your hearts. We have wronged no one, we have corrupted no one, we have exploited no one. I do not say this to condemn you; I have said before that you have such a place in our hearts that we would live or die with you. (2 Corinthians 7:2-3)

The concept of accountability inevitably arises when a small group ministry forms. Whether it is pairing off with a prayer partner or a small Bible study group, accountability is often held up as a good reason to get involved. But is accountability such a great thing? Is it something we can expect from every small group or friendship? What does healthy accountability look like anyway?

Accountability Must Be Preceded by Relationship

Accountability is based on a preexisting relationship. For example, an employee is accountable to his employer. Because of their relationship the employer has the right to correct or question the employee's work whenever he deems necessary. In the same way, the Christians in Corinth were accountable to Paul because of his role in establishing the church.

Indeed, many had become Christians through his personal ministry. It was this preexisting friendship that made them accountable to Paul.

It is foolhardy to think that you can be accountable to just anyone, Christian or not. Healthy accountability requires that a trusted relationship be established first. While meeting with a prayer partner may allow a friendship to grow, it won't guarantee the right conditions for accountability. Wisdom dictates that you allow time to test such a new relationship before you place yourself in a position of accountability.

Accountability Stays within Appropriate Boundaries

Have you ever known a friend who seemed to be trying to live your life for you? Perhaps she had the diagnosis for all your problems, or she continually checked up on your decisions. Such friendship is usually smothered to death early on. It certainly doesn't reflect God's design for accountability.

Accountability implies boundaries. If you've received medication from your doctor, you expect him to follow up your recovery. But should he ask you about another area of your life unrelated to your medical concerns, you might take offense. When we retort, "That's none of your business," we are affirming that accountability has boundaries.

Paul talked pointedly to the Corinthians about two concerns: 1) their painful accusations against him and 2) their pagan practices that were warping their walk with Christ. Both of these areas were well within Paul's sphere of responsibility. He avoided confrontation on differences of opinion. For example, Paul clearly identified his single lifestyle as being one of personal preference. Paul mandated neither marriage nor singleness for Christians (see 1 Corinthians 7:7-9, 25-40).

Like Paul, we all have a right to our opinions. We can share our opinions as our advice is sought. But we must remember that even in the best of friendships, life is largely a matter of perspective. Only when we are asked to keep a friend specifically accountable do we have the right to do so. And should a friend decide to no longer be held accountable in some area, we should respect the new boundary as well.

Prayer and Accountability Go Together

Accountability gets sticky because friendships are largely subjective experiences. You may feel close to someone and think you can trust them. You may want them to know about a struggle you are having. As you share, it is only natural for your friend to likewise express concern.

This is where prayer can be such a help. It might happen like this. A close friend and I are concluding a visit. I ask, "I was wondering if you would want to spend a few minutes in prayer before I leave?" This is an invitation to deepen our relationship. It is also an invitation to accountability. If she agrees, a short conversation will take place during which we will share specific prayer requests.

"I'm worried about my mom's failing health," she says. Or perhaps she'll mention her son's problems at school, financial difficulties or even more personal concerns. I listen, and in turn, voice my own concerns, then through prayer our concerns are voiced again to God. As I think of my friend in the days to come, I'll continue to pray for her. I may even give her a call to see how she is doing. It will only be natural for me to inquire about her concerns the next time we are together. This is biblical accountability in action.

The relationship between prayer and accountability is reflected in the verse:

> Therefore confess your sins to each other
> and pray for each other so that you may
> be healed. The prayer of a righteous man
> is powerful and effective. (James 5:16)

If I only talk about my sins, I am being honest, but not accountable. By inviting a friend to pray with me, I am entering a threefold pledge for change. As the confessing friend, I am admitting before her that my sins need to be forsaken. Second, I am acknowledging that God is able to help effect change. Last, I am implying a humble willingness to forsake my sin and obey God.

For my listening friend, praying together also becomes a threefold responsibility. First, she needs to respond in faithful prayer. Second, she must be willing to hold the confession in confidence. Third, she should demonstrate accountability by occasionally asking me about my request.

Although accountability is simply an agreement between two people, Christian accountability is different. For Christians, accountability is an agreement among three persons: me, my friend and God. What begins in conversation is strengthened by promises and is cemented by God's presence in prayer. And while everyday accountability may keep us in line, accountability that springs from prayer changes lives. Who can tell what God will do when we come together in honest confession of our needs for Him, commit ourselves to obedience and pray for one another?

If you don't have a prayer partner, I urge you to begin seeking one. Accountability apart from prayer ultimately rests on your own resolution. Prayerful accountability rests on the immeasurable power of God.

Accountability Is a Two-Way Street

Making ourselves accountable through confession and prayer should be a partnership. At the very least, the listening partner is accountable to pray for the confessing partner. Likewise the one confessing is accountable to take steps of obedience. Both are accountable to God first, and to one another second.

Have you ever had a friend say to you, "Thanks for praying. You'll never believe what happened, . . ." then they proceed to share some exciting answer to prayer? The only problem is that you didn't remember to pray. Now you are faced with a dilemma. Do you reveal your faithlessness to your friend and risk offending her, or do you just rejoice with her and not mention that you failed to pray? Regardless of your decision, the invisible inner prick of conscience reminds you that accountability is indeed a two-way street.

In contrast, a professional relationship is one-sided with regard to accountability between the counselor and the client. It's not that professionals can do without accountability, but the client/counselor relationship is not the right place for such sharing to take place. Accountability between friends, however, fares best with a mutual exchange of concerns, needs and secrets.

Accountability and Secrets: What to Tell and What to Keep

How do secrets fit into accountability? By secrets, I mean the personal ones that originate with you. When should a secret be shared with a trusted friend, a professional counselor or kept to yourself?

There is no doubt that telling secrets in confidence is an important part of friendship. Through trust and honesty, we can best experience the benefits of being accountable to another. While some secrets may best be reserved for the ears of a professional, most secrets can be shared in a trusted friendship.

However, remember that while secrets can bind hearts together, they can also wreak havoc if not handled carefully. Nothing can end a friendship quicker than a betrayed confidence. James describes the power of the tongue as being like a match tossed carelessly into dry underbrush. One small spark out of place, and a raging forest fire is underway (see James 3:6). We must control our tongues if we want to preserve intimate friendships. On our own, this would be impossible (3:2). Yet we serve a God who will enable us to keep our vows of secrecy. But if we don't intend to look to Him for help in keeping those vows, then we shouldn't promise our confidence.

So how can we know which secrets to tell and which to keep? What may work well as a guideline for one may seem inappropriate for another. If you are in doubt, ask God for wisdom in choosing a confidante. With this disclaimer in mind, consider the following guidelines in sharing confidences.

1. Choose Your Confidante Carefully

Avoid sharing secrets with someone who is in a position to use that information against you. I usually discourage ministry wives from taking other staff wives into confidence. Why? If their friendship ruptures, the offended confidante could use the secrets to bring great harm. We'd like to think back stabbing and gossip don't happen within the church, but the testimonies of those who have been brutalized by wagging tongues urge us toward caution. The same caution applies to the workplace.

2. Confide in a Neutral Friend

One beautiful spring day my husband and I were carving out some new flower beds in our front yard. I had decided that my yard would look like something from *Better Homes and Gardens* that summer. I could almost visualize the beautiful flowers I'd have. However, sore muscles put a damper on my enthusiasm, and I called for a break long enough to collect the mail. In the mailbox was a letter inviting my husband to apply for what appeared to be a ministry position perfectly tailored to his desires. The letter informed us that the candidating process would begin within a month. Lord willing, the decision would be made by July, with the goal that the new pastor would start work in September. My mental *Better Homes and Gardens* vision evaporated. A vision of packing boxes, difficult partings, awkward adjustments and loneliness replaced it.

I was emotionally overwhelmed at the thought of leaving. At first I tried to carry my burden alone, but it was too heavy. My heart was breaking and I couldn't pretend it wasn't. I knew I needed to pray with someone. I needed to surrender this burden to the Lord in the presence of an unbiased Christian outside of my denomination. In tears, I confessed my need to God. I also promised to surrender this burden publicly by responding to an altar call should God want me to do so.

Several days later I attended an evening service at my friend Pam's church. I had come primarily to witness her baptism. I'd almost forgotten my prayer a few days earlier. But God hadn't. After the baptism, the pastor preached a sermon that seemed to be directed right at me. Then almost as an afterthought he closed the evening service with an altar call. I knew what I needed to do even though I dreaded it.

God, what will people think? I countered mentally. *I've written books. I've spoken at retreats. They will think I'm some kind of awful sinner if I go forward.* But the Holy Spirit wouldn't let me forget my promise, and He wouldn't let me overlook this opportunity.

I fumbled my way awkwardly to the aisle and started toward the front. I don't know what people thought. I may have been the only one to come forward that night. I know I was the first. But I also knew I needed to surrender my home and family to God as I faced this new opportunity.

The pastor met me at the end of the aisle. "I haven't come to receive Christ," I explained brokenly. "I just need someone to pray with." Within moments I found myself in a side room facing a couple I'd never met. Rich and Barbara were a retired navy couple. Few could understand the pain of moving better than they did. They had also been in ministry for a short time. God couldn't have chosen better confidantes for the occasion. My dear friend, Pam, joined us as well. As we prayed, I yielded my situation to God for Him to do as He thought best. Immediately a peace settled over my mind. I was still terribly sad at the thought of leaving, but God was in control again. I no longer needed to carry my burden alone.

Would sharing my secret with someone from my own church have been wrong? Not necessarily. But the anonymity of this situation enabled me to share with greater security. If there was any gossip about my confession that night, it wouldn't have jeopardized my husband's current ministry.

3. Don't Gossip in the Name of Accountability

Confessing a need almost often requires explaining circumstances involving another person. A healthy confession explains the facts pertinent to the need for prayer. Identifying when we are telling more than we ought to is hard. It is this tension over separating the necessary facts from the unnecessary that has given many prayer chains a reputation for gossip.

Gossip is largely an issue of motivation. People use gossip to place themselves at the center of attention instead of the prayer request. They also use it to effect revenge against another. One author wrote, "Gossip allows individuals to say otherwise private things without taking responsibility" (Levin and Arluke 1987, 22).

Such uses of confession are wrong. The book of Proverbs is full of warnings about the damage that gossip does to relationships. Perhaps you know of marriages, careers or friendships that were damaged this way. Instead, we need to make David's prayer our own:

> May my prayer be set before you like
>   incense;
>   may the lifting up of my hands be like
>   the evening sacrifice.
> Set a guard over my mouth, O Lord;
>   keep watch over the door of my lips.
>   (Psalm 141:2-3)

4. Don't Expect Friends to Be Professional Counselors

Friends are great treasures. If they are able to occasionally give us wise counsel, such friendships can shape our lives in powerful ways. Blessed is the person who has such resources to go to at times of confusion.

But listening to a friend's confidence can also become burdensome. It takes a lot of emotional energy to share another's hurt. We all have only so much of that energy to go around. While Galatians 6:2 urges us to "carry each other's burdens", the same passage also notes "for each one should carry his own load" (6:5). God's plan for friendship is that we help one another out in a bind. It is also His plan that the hurting friend take responsibility for himself in the day-to-day struggles. God doesn't intend Christian compassion to support irresponsibility on the part of another.

Kim was late and openly irritated as we took our seats at a local cafe for lunch. She explained what was troubling her. "This gal from my church keeps calling and asking for prayer," Kim began. "She keeps going on and on about her problems. I try to give her counsel, but she won't accept it. When I try to cut her off she acts hurt. I feel badly. I suppose she has no one else to talk to, but I have things to do, too. That's why I'm late today, she wouldn't let me get off the phone!"

Does Kim's predicament sound familiar? The world is full of needy people; some are more needy than others. Kim's caller wanted emotional support that Kim was no longer able to provide. Perhaps you've had a friend like Kim's. Or perhaps you are the one in need. It helps to realize that God doesn't expect all the world's problems to fall on one person's shoulders. That is why He describes the church as a body. It is also His design that some Christians be better equipped to minister to those needing emotional support and counsel. John Townsend and Henry Cloud observed:

We all need more than God and a best friend. We need a group of supportive relationships. The reason is simple: having more than one person in our lives allows our friends to be human. To be busy. To be unavailable at times. To hurt and have problems of their own. To have time alone. (Townsend & Cloud, 1992, 111)

We can't expect our friends to take the place of professional counselors. We can ask for their perspective on a situation. We can ask them to pray. But emotional litterbugs soon wear out their welcome. As Proverbs 25:17 warns: "Seldom set foot in your neighbor's house—too much of you, and he will hate you."

5. Don't Share Things That Will Wound

Alice once told me about a conversation she had with her elderly aunt. Because she was afflicted with Alzheimer's disease, Aunt Lily was living with Alice and her family. One day Aunt Lily confused Alice with her sister, Trudy. Thinking she was talking to Trudy, Aunt Lily proceeded to tell Alice all the things she didn't like about her. It was quite an eye-opening conversation!

Most of us can't claim Aunt Lily's excuse for being so insensitive. It is wrong to bring up a secret shared in the past to wield as a sword in the present. It is equally wrong to share secret thoughts and feelings that will undermine the relationship. I remember hearing about a man who, when asked by his wife if he ever thought about other women, responded by describing his fantasies. No wonder she went into a jealous rage. What he thought was honesty was really irresponsible disclosure. The only time we should use secrets to wound is when bold confrontation is needed to enable a stagnated relationship to heal. Even then, such confrontation should be a last resort.

6. Secrecy Can Be a Heavy Burden

Think twice before sharing information that may involve a secret too heavy for your friend to carry. If you've been the keeper of some dark secret over the years, you'll know what I mean. Such secrets should be shared only when necessary, and only with friends that really need to hear them. We must also consider whether this secret is an unfair burden to ask them to carry. We may be asking too much especially if the secret conceals wrong. Some such secrets may even implicate the hearer legally. Even professional counselors cannot protect that kind of confidence. If you need to confess such secrets, I urge you to consider talking to a counselor and letting your friends off the hook.

Is Accountability Worth the Risk?

Developing healthy accountability in several trusted friendships is hard. It is so hard we may be tempted to ask whether such a dimension to friendship is really worthwhile. Isn't account-ability just too risky? The answer to both questions is a resounding "Yes".

Accountability is risky and it carries the potential to damage a friendship. Advice can be rejected or misinterpreted. Secrets told in confidence can be betrayed. It is the incredible dividends that make accountability worth pursuing. Kindred spirits know this is part of what binds them together. More importantly, accountability is part of God's design for Christian friendship.

Someone once said Christians should relate like a bunch of grapes. As they get handled by life, they should rub up against one another, bruise one another and spill their sweetness onto one another. In reality, however, Christians tend to relate more like a bag of marbles than a bunch of grapes. Many are hard and self-contained, bouncing off one another with little effect. Yet grapes, not marbles, are the reality God desires our friendships to reflect. In fact, from Acts to Revelation it is clear that the church is to be accountable.

Accountability also plays an important role in our health. In a fascinating book, *Opening Up,* Dr. James W. Pennebaker writes of a study he did on the physiological effects of confiding in others. The results are amazing. There was a direct correlation between unconfessed secrets and ill health. His secular study highlights

what James 5:16 has long advised: accountability and healing go together.

Accountability can give us new perspectives
on life. Proverbs 15:22 says: "Plans fail for lack
of counsel, but with many advisers they succeed." Counsel can't be equated with accountability, but it is certainly part of the process.
You'll be a more successful person if you have a
wise friend for a counselor.

Accountability can also spare us from spiritual
shipwreck. One author summed it up this way:

> No one can survive his own unchallenged
> authority. Every true, committed Chris-
> tian in a leadership role needs to submit
> himself and his ideas to other mature be-
> lievers who will hold him accountable.
> (Anderson 1990, 164)

Accountable friendships help us get rid of
pride and stay grounded spiritually.

Last, accountability deepens friendships.
King Solomon grasped this well when he
wrote:

> Perfume and incense bring joy to the
>   heart,
>   and the pleasantness of one's friend
> springs from his earnest counsel. (Prov-
> erbs 27:9)

Remember Paul sitting in Ephesus and sadly
describing his heartache to his friends in
Corinth? Accountability had pushed their

friendship nearly to the breaking point. Was it worth the risk? Read the results for yourself:

> See what this godly sorrow has produced in you: what earnestness, what eagerness to clear yourselves, what indignation, what alarm, what longing, what concern, what readiness to see justice done. At every point you have proved yourselves to be innocent in this matter. So even though I wrote to you, it was not on account of the one who did the wrong or of the injured party, but rather that before God you could see for yourselves how devoted to us you are. By all this we are encouraged. (2 Corinthians 7:11-13)

Making It Yours

1. Do you have a friend that you've been accountable to? How has accountability impacted your friendship? How has it impacted your life?

2. Read Genesis 18:20-32 and Numbers 14:1-24. What were the results of Abraham's and Moses' intercessory prayers? How do these stories highlight the power of prayer mentioned in James 5:16-18?

3. Biblical accountability involves making a threefold pledge for change on the confessor's part. What are the three parts of that pledge?

4. Biblical accountability also involves the listener in a threefold responsibility. List the three responsibilities involved in receiving another's confession.

5. List the six guidelines for sharing secrets.

_____

_____

_____

_____

_____

_____

Which guideline seemed most relevant to your life or offered new insight? Why?

6. God's design for friendship includes that Christians be accountable to one another. This truth has been illustrated as the difference between a bunch of grapes and a bag of marbles. Which of these two illustrations best represents your relational style?

7. Accountability is risky. Do you think it is worth the risk? Explain.

Chapter 9

Friendship Close to Home

With red puffy eyes and a quivering lower lip, Sierra stood before me bemoaning her fate.

"It's an honor to be chosen to play Mary in the Christmas program," I explained patiently. "All you have to do is sit up there and look holy. You'll do fine."

"But I don't want to be Mary! At first I said I'd do it, but now I've changed my mind," Sierra protested.

"Why would it be so awful?" I inquired further, a bit exasperated.

"Someone said, 'I'm sure glad I don't have to be Mary. Daniel's UGLY!' And now I have to stand next to him as Mary." Then, assured that she was on the path to public humiliation, Sierra again burst into a flood of tears.

I did my best to stifle a smile and wondered how a lanky, freckled third grade boy could ever appear ugly. "Who told you that?" I probed.

"His sister!" Sierra reported with emphasis.

"Well, what would you expect from a sister? I sincerely doubt Daniel is ugly. But I suppose the original Mary may have had some of the same misgivings about her Joseph that you are having. The difference is that for her, the arrangement was permanent, and she probably had no say." Then I shared a similar experience when I was Mary in a Christmas pageant appearing opposite a Joseph I wasn't too sure of either.

"How did you feel?" Sierra sniffed, as she contemplated the possibility that her mother had survived such a fate.

"I recall feeling much the way you did. I was very nervous, but also a little excited. The boy picked for Joseph was pretty wild, but I also thought he was kinda cute."

Somehow that amazing confession filled Sierra with the strength to later don her sheets, pick up her baby doll and fulfill her role as Mary in the annual Christmas pageant. Daniel, clad in a bathrobe, dutifully knelt beside her—close enough to be considered a couple, but just barely.

A History of Marital Friendship

Perhaps Sierra and Daniel weren't that unlike the original Mary and Joseph . We know that Joseph was compassionate toward Mary. When he learned that Mary was pregnant, he planned to divorce her privately rather than make the divorce a public spectacle. But the blend of compassion and faith we see in the introductory remarks in Matthew and Luke hardly describes a deep, abiding friendship. The truth is that most marriages throughout history were rather passionless. Prior to Christ women were largely viewed in subservient positions. Marriages were arranged for financial or political gain, for producing heirs to preserve the family line and for managing a man's estate. Friendship between husband and wife might eventually characterize a marriage, but it certainly wasn't expected. Instead, couples fell into their prescribed social roles and the cycle of birth, life and death rolled onward. It was only as a result of the teachings of Christ that the wife was elevated to full, equal standing with her husband. That was why it was necessary for Paul to admonish the Christian wife to submit to her husband, and for a Christian husband to actively love his wife (see Ephesians 5). The way Christian couples treated each other was evidence of their conversion. These were radically new social concepts.

Through the cross men and women have equal worth (see Galatians 3:28). It may be hard for us to appreciate the radical impact of this message but it was truly revolutionary. In Jesus' day, for example, divorce was a singularly male privilege. A husband could legally dismiss his wife for any reason, and she had no recourse.

The role of women has changed dramatically over the years. With the advent of the 20th century, new options were offered to western women. In 1919 women earned the right to vote.

As a result of World Wars I and II, women were thrust from the home into the workplace where they earned respect as providers. Educational opportunities followed. Today few professions are without female employees.

In addition the average lifespan has been extended. In the old days, few had the time to waste on extramarital affairs much less mid-life crises. Indeed, it is only with the modern era that many of the relational issues facing marriages have arisen.

These changes have made it necessary for couples to attend seriously to their marriages. No longer is marriage an inviolate contract held together by social pressure. The result for many is that marriage has become a choice regulated by the quality of the marriage relationship.

Why Lovers Need to Be Friends

Reason #1: *Friendship Protects Marriages*

We all know that adultery is wrong. Many spouses can't imagine themselves ever being wooed away by another. "That would never happen to us," Kay says confidently. "Besides, we are committed to each another. I know Joe would never think of fooling around." But her confidence may be ungrounded if she and Joe are not investing in the friendship their marriage offers. It certainly is ungrounded if their primary emotional investments are being made elsewhere.

While we may be quick to condemn adultery, many people see no harm in building their closest friendships outside of their marriages. The early disillusionments of married life often convince a spouse that her chosen mate is incapable of becoming her best friend. For example, a friend at work may seem to understand these feelings. She may share the same interests, values and concerns. Often it is all too easy to begin making the emotional investments in the friendhip like this alone. Perhaps her mate has chosen to do the same. Neglected, the marriage relationship withers. What started out as a passionate promise with the highest of hopes becomes routine and lifeless. They talk less. They spend less time together. Before long, the marriage resembles little more than a roommate arrangement. Intimacy has died. And because society no longer honors marriage as a lifetime commitment, divorce seems an acceptable solution.

But divorce need not be the only solution for a dying relationship. Instead, nurture your marriage into a warm, committed friendship. Such a relationship is not only a rich blessing, but is also the greatest protection from the undermining attitudes and temptations of the world. As one author wrote, "Marriages usually don't collapse overnight. They become bankrupt gradually because they lack daily deposits of love, communication, and affirmation" (Fields, 1991, 15). Every couple needs to realize that nurturing their marriage friendship is an insurance policy they can't do without.

Reason #2: *Friendship Is God's Plan for Marriage*

God's plan for marriage is another reason marriage needs to evolve into friendship. Adam's aloneness was the only aspect of God's creation deemed incomplete. Thus, Eve was lovingly created to meet Adam's relational needs (see Genesis 2:18). But their marriage amounted to more than Eve's role versus Adam's. In fact, neither Adam nor Eve even thought about who should take out the trash, mow the lawn or do the dishes. Roles were irrelevant before they sinned. Instead, unity was the object of their relationship.

As the first couple came together they surrendered their separate identities to discover a union made of their strengths, weaknesses, likes and dislikes. Adam and Eve became a team. Their mission was to rule the world. It wasn't until Adam and Eve were disobedient that it was necessary to designate roles in marriage. Cooperation, not competition, reigns where perfect love exists. In the beginning, Adam and Eve's bond of friendship ruled their hearts making role definitions unnecessary.

Today wives need to be reminded to love and respect their husbands. Husbands need to be reminded to lovingly care for their wives. A growing friendship and individual roles for the husband and wife remain part of God's plan for marriage. Unlike roles, however, friendship cannot be commanded into existence. God leaves the nurturing of such a dimension to us.

Reason #3: *Friendship Leads to Maturity*

Someone wrote: "Romance talks about love; friendship puts it to the ultimate test" (Kinder & Cowan, 1989, 172). How true! It's one thing to be emotionally stirred by dreams of marital bliss prior to marriage, and something else to live with the differences married life soon uncovers. After all, how were you to know that your mate would insist on sleeping with the windows wide open or that his idea of hanging up clothes was a heap in the corner of the bedroom? How was he supposed to know that when you were upset, you needed a soft hug and listening ear but NOT solutions? Indeed, the differences married life reveals can seem so great that many couples wonder how they ever got together in the first place. This is where friendship can make or break the relationship. The decision must be made to either adapt to one another and work things through, or to wallow in disillusionment and make emotional investments elsewhere.

In this way the adjustments of marriage give a unique opportunity to mature. After all, few best friends could endure living together. In spite of their warm compatibility, their differences would eventually drive them apart. Only a marriage bound by a solid promise of loyalty before God and one another can carry two people through this difficult maturing process. Marriage offers the opportunity to develop elements of character (patience, self-control, long-suffering, loyalty) which are left undeveloped by less demanding friendships. Granted, the life-shaping conflicts of marriage are far from comfortable, but worked through in God's strength, such marriage conflicts offer a sure path to maturity.

Reason #4: *Friendship Expands Your Horizons*

Do you remember the Greek myth about Narcissus? He was such an arrogant, self-absorbed youth that he spurned all offers of love. Then one day he sat down to rest at the edge of a spring and caught his reflection in the water. He was so enthralled with the beauty of his own image that he was unable to leave. Instead, he sat there gazing into the pool until he wasted away into the flower that now bears his name.

The moral seems as clear as Narcissus' reflection: Self absorption stunts the personality and ultimately destroys it. None of us is strong enough to live as an island. What God said for Adam applies to all mankind: "It is not good for the man to be alone" (Genesis 2:18). Friendship helps to provide balance in life and saves us from undue introspection.

Narcissus had a friend whose name was Echo. Echo was a nymph who was only able to parrot what another said. It was a comfortable relationship because it made for few differences. Then one day she followed Narcissus on a hunting trip into the mountains. When he fell into trouble, Narcissus called for help. Echo answered but was unable to give him the counsel he needed. In the end, Narcissus forsook Echo. Heartbroken, Echo stayed in the mountains mourning for Narcissus until only her voice was left.

It is our differences that make marital friendship both a challenge and rare blessing. He was raised in suburbia. She grew up in the country. He was a firstborn child in a family of four. She was the third in a family of six. His parents were Catholic. She never went to church until high school. He likes to camp and fish. She likes to shop.

These are just some of the differences marriage uncovers. When the fires of initial romance have cooled, rediscovering common ground can prove to be challenging. Instead of drawing us into new experiences, we often allow differences like these to repel us. It is easy to see how common interests build quick friendships. There is nothing wrong with having friends who enjoy the same things you do. But friendships based on commonality alone lack opportunities for growth. The world is full of enriching new experiences and perspectives to be embraced with an adventurous, open spirit. Many of these experiences are possible through the differences between spouses. The trick is to make such differences bridges instead of barriers.

My husband took me golfing on our honeymoon. After several frustrating holes and countless minutes in the weeds searching for my ball, I very dramatically threw down my club, burst into tears and announced that I would never play this "stupid" game again. I haven't either. But I have learned to caddy. Walking with my husband over a manicured course, I've come to appreciate the landscaping and the expertise that golfing requires. You might find this hard to believe, but sometimes I'll even watch a little golf on TV. I still have no desire to golf and I'm sure course owners are relieved by the news. But this is just one example of how we were able to make a difference into a bridge instead of a barrier. Whatever your differences, you can do the same. Provided your mate's interests are not sinful, you too can compromise to expand your horizons. You'll be richer for doing so.

Are the differences between you and your spouse becoming barriers? Are you tempted to dream of a mate more like yourself? Ask God to give you a new perspective because the differences in a loving friendship can enrich and broaden life. As the ancient Greek myth of

Echo and Narcissus illustrates, we need other perspectives to guide and enrich our lives.

Reason #5: *Friendship Brings Depth to a Relationship*

While books and seminars on improving marriage abound, comparatively little attention is given to the friendship aspect of marriage. Yet friendship with a spouse affects every aspect of the relationship. As two professional counselors noted: "Love, in the absence of friendship, is only a hormonal illusion. One cannot desire another person over the long haul without really being friends with him or her" (Kinder & Cowan, 1989, 166). It is friendship that gives enduring strength and warmth to marriage.

Reality Check

I hesitated to write this chapter because so many live with difficult marriages. The concept of befriending a mate may appear impossible. Therefore, before examining the building blocks for marital friendship, consider these four perspectives to help you connect your reality with the ideal marriage Scripture presents.

1. First, remember that God's perfect model for marriage depicted in the Bible isn't meant to discourage us. Instead, He wants to show us how much we need His help. Our friendship with God should always be our most intimate relationship. We need to draw on the strength

He has promised us to live as He has designed. Without Him, fully experiencing God's design for marriage is impossible.

2. Another primary truth of Scripture is that growth is a process. Achieving a close marital friendship does not happen overnight. We must become sensitive to God's leading through the Holy Spirit in order to learn how to cultivate friendship with our mate. Being open to opportunities for friendship as they present themselves indicates a willingness to follow God's leading in this process. A good marital friendship takes a lifetime of learning but the learning isn't a static uphill climb. Life is lived in phases of intimacy or independence and in periods of success or failure. So don't immediately despair if your spouse seems unresponsive to your offers of friendship. A change for the better may be right around the corner.

3. Individual freedom is another truth highlighted by Scripture. While it is true that friendship can be encouraged, it can not be forced. Despite all your efforts, your mate may be incapable or unwilling to return your friendship. If this is the case, I encourage you to surrender your heartache to God and look to Him for the grace to make the best of things. Remember, success isn't having a perfect marriage. For your marriage, it may mean struggling to stay, forgive and invest as long as God directs. You are not faithful to one another on the strength

of your own passions. Ultimately, if you are faithful to God, He will enable you to be faithful to your mate.

4. Last, remember nothing is impossible for God. Your closest friend is the One who can work miracles. If you find yourself in a difficult marriage, go to God in prayer. Ask Him for wisdom and obey His leading. You can't change your mate, but you can change yourself—and that's 50 percent of your marriage relationship. A change like that is bound to have an impact.

Becoming Your Mate's Best Friend

With these perspectives in mind, how is a deeper friendship encouraged within a marriage? The answer is really very simple. Do many of the same things you would do to encourage a friendship with someone else. Start by building memories.

Memory Making

How long has it been since you've done something special together? Friendships are built on investments of time that turn into treasured memories. In his helpful book, *Creative Romance,* Doug Fields shares his philosophy for marital dating: "My wife and I are sure to have disappointing episodes and some regretful moments. But one of our goals is to make sure that our positive memories outweigh our heartaches" (Fields, 1991, 19). What a great goal! But the mental photo albums of many couples hold only bitter recollections. After collecting a few pages of such experiences, they give up or begin building positive memories with others.

Disappointment is always bitter. Perhaps you can recall a time you and your husband planned an evening away only to have everything fall apart. If expectations had been high, the disappointment was probably a crushing blow. Satan would love for this disappointment to become bitter disillusionment. "Why go to the effort to plan an evening out?" he whispers. "You remember what happened last time." All too often, Satan's verdict is accepted without investing further in the relationship.

But it is possible to transform many disappointments into fun memories. I remember one couple recounting their first camping trip. The retelling of the disastrous weekend was so funny we laughed until we cried. True, they never became veteran campers, but they had succeeded in turning a bitter experience into a fun memory. How we view life ultimately boils down to a matter of perspective. Satan's perspective is always a shrinking, bitter, pessimistic outlook. The perspective of faith trusts God to heal the past and bring a brighter tomorrow.

Another reason couples quit dating is that they seem to have less and less to talk about. The awkward silence between them is uncomfortable. Many times, it seems easier to stay apart than face the emotional reality of their dying relationship. If this resembles your situation, start by doing something small together. Watch sports on TV together, go to a movie or concert or do something with your children or another couple. Stay away from situations that require sustained conversation or deteriorate into undue introspection. Instead start small, and try not to expect too much, too soon.

If you are in a relationship where you have little to say to one another, intimacy has virtually died. You really need to begin afresh to build your marital friendship. Provide simple, nonthreatening memories at the beginning. This is the first step to building a friendship with anyone else. Chances are it will work with your spouse as well. Then as you rediscover one another, you can move on to planning bigger experiences together.

Probably one of the biggest blockades to marital dating is that couples don't enjoy doing the same things. Before you were married, you may have gone along with your husband's interests. He may have gone along with yours. You both wanted to impress each other with how loving and flexible you were. After a few years of marriage, you may be sick of "going along" and are ready to reveal that you despise fishing, shopping or whatever.

Having your own interests isn't wrong. Couples that are best friends don't necessarily do everything together. The challenge is to discover new interests that both can share such as the kids' sporting events or a new hobby. Suddenly your interests broaden and you've found a way to build another memory.

Practice Forgiving

Forgiveness is difficult because it is so costly. Someone must bear the consequences for the wrong that has taken place. Christ bore the pain of our sin when He died on the cross. If Jesus wanted revenge, He would now be making us suffer for the pain our sin caused Him. Instead, Jesus drew on God's grace to bear the sting of sin and extended to us His unreserved love and forgiveness. Without His attitude of grace, friendship with Christ would be impossible.

Paul said this is the same attitude we are to imitate when approaching earthly relationships. It is impossible to do on our own. None of us can extend the same forgiveness that Christ did. Such attitudes are foreign to our self-centered nature. Yet when we allow God to change our hearts, He has promised to help us treat one another with the attitudes that build rather than destroy.

Tracy and Martin had been married for nine years. They hadn't been easy years either. Financial stress was a constant burden. Even after advanced training and several job changes, Martin's career still seemed headed nowhere. With three small children underfoot, Tracy began to long for some sense of permanence and security in their lives. Instead, what began as willing sacrifices on her part faded into a bitter cycle of high hopes and disappointments. Tracy's disillusionment fueled Martin's frustration. When she tried to express her feelings, he felt accused by her unhappiness. She, in turn, felt neglected, unappreciated and misunderstood. Conversation between them dribbled to a near standstill. Increasingly, they spent their time in different worlds. Tracy was involved with the children. Martin was lost in his work. Although both were Christians, Tracy finally had to face the bleak future of her marriage if something didn't change. "I don't know how much longer I can stand it," she confided to a friend. "I don't love him anymore. We argue all the time. If the right guy came along and showed some interest in me, I know I'd leave."

Like many, Martin's and Tracy's marriage might easily have ended in divorce. Instead Tracy allowed the Holy Spirit to make a difference. She realized she couldn't change Martin. But she could allow God to change her, and that's where Tracy began. This decision was a significant step in saving her marriage.

Next Tracy began talking with a Christian counselor. Under the counselor's direction, Tracy uncovered personal insights and found the accountability she needed to reinvest in the marriage. There were no easy cures. There usually never are. But as the Holy Spirit began to mold Tracy, Martin also became attentive. For the first time in years, he wanted to listen to Tracy's needs and focus more energy on their relationship. She, in turn, began to share her needs without a critical and defensive attitude.

Martin and Tracy survived the disillusionments of marriage because they focused first on Christ. Through His Word and godly counsel they were able to change their attitudes and, in turn, heal their marriage. Today Martin and Tracy enjoy a close friendship and are together confronting the joys and hardships life presents.

Does the testimony above strike a sympathetic chord within you? Working through past hurts to renew a relationship is tough, complicated work. You may want to consider talking to a counselor as Tracy did or reading books written by experienced counselors. The titles of several books on communication in marriage are listed at the end of this chapter. Purchase several (or borrow from a local or church library) and prayerfully read them. We serve an all powerful God who wants your marriage to not only succeed, but also to blossom into friendship. Don't give up before you give Him a chance.

Actions Speak Louder Than Words

On your wedding day you and your mate exchanged vows. Together you solemnly promised to love, honor and cherish one another. But if a hidden camera were to record a week in your home, what would the record show? Ultimately, it is our actions that speak the loudest. It is one thing to promise our love, and yet another thing to act loving.

Wedged between two immense volumes of Jewish history, the small book of Ruth holds a tender picture of marital friendship. Ruth met and married her first husband in her native land of Moab. After his death, she left Moab to live in Judah with her mother-in-law. Both widowed, they settled in Bethlehem, and Ruth soon began working as a gleaner in the fields.

Gleaners would walk behind the reapers to collect any grain that was dropped. Portions of the field were also left for the gleaners to harvest. This practice was outlined in the Law as God's provision for the needy, especially widows (see Leviticus 19:9-10). However, having the legal right to reap was where the gleaner's protection ended. The Law didn't specify how much should be left for the needy. No doubt, many owners made it difficult for the gleaners to collect a day's wage. It is certain that they were often the targets of verbal and sometimes physical abuse.

God had guided Ruth to Boaz's field. When Boaz arrived at the field, he noticed Ruth and asked one of the servants about her. "She is the Moabitess who came back from Moab with Naomi," the servant replied. "She went into the field and has worked steadily from morning till now, except for a short rest in the shelter" (Ruth 2:6-7).

Next, Boaz addresses Ruth personally. "My daughter, listen to me," he says kindly. "Don't go and glean in another field and don't go away from here. Stay here with my servant girls. Watch the field where the men are harvesting, and follow along after the girls. I have told the men not to touch you. And whenever you are thirsty, go and get a drink from the water jars the men have filled" (2:8-9).

In these few words, Boaz demonstrated extraordinary kindness to Ruth. What a comfort on the first day of gleaning, that Boaz, an esteemed landowner in Bethlehem, offered his welcome and protection to her. She was also invited to drink from the water supply whenever she needed to. This may not seem like a big kindness to us, but in a hot land where water was in limited supply and had to be drawn by hand, access to drinking water was a privilege.

Boaz's kindness overwhelmed Ruth. Bowing down before him, she asked the obvious question: "Why have I found such favor in your eyes that you notice me—a foreigner?" (2:10).

Boaz responded, "I've been told all about what you have done for your mother-in-law since the death of your husband" (2:11). Then he gave to Ruth a special blessing: "May the LORD repay you for what you have done. May you be richly rewarded by the LORD, the God of Israel, under whose wings you have come to take refuge" (2:12).

If only everyone could hear such encouragement on their first day of work! Ruth could hardly believe it herself. "May I continue to find favor in your eyes, my lord," she said to Boaz. "You have given me comfort and have spoken kindly to your servant—though I do not have the standing of one of your servant girls" (2:13).

But Boaz wasn't finished. Later he invited her to join his harvest crew in a meal. Boaz even served her personally. When she returned to work, Boaz instructed the harvesters to leave extra grain for her and prohibited them from embarrassing her in any way.

Is it any wonder that Ruth stayed in Boaz's field the rest of the harvest season? Is it any wonder that she later asked him to marry her? Boaz was much older. Even by his own words, he didn't consider himself a desirable mate for young Ruth (3:10). Yet after watching Boaz, and receiving his kindnesses day after day, Ruth was ready to risk the misunderstanding her forwardness might produce.

So often we think of big, dramatic gifts when we think of demonstrating our love—a dozen roses, a romantic dinner in a fine restaurant, an expensive vacation, etc. But it is really the little daily gestures that keep a friendship alive: things like compliments or helping out when you can. It's a touch that communicates comfort or esteem. Kindness includes making time together a priority, rather than giving your spouse the leftovers of your day. It is going that little bit extra when it's unexpected. Surprise dates gifts can be fun. But the warmth of a friendship is largely built on the multitude of the little considerate acts sown throughout the years.

Words Have Power, Too

Words have incredible power to build or destroy. Through our conversation, we can bring out the best or worst in one another. It's no surprise that Paul mentions conversation in his passage on relationships in Ephesians. He wrote: "Do not let any unwholesome talk come out of your mouths, but only what is helpful for building others up according to their needs, that it may benefit those who listen" (Ephesians 4:29). Every Christian needs to memorize and apply this counsel. For if we only spoke what was helpful, needful and timely, we could avoid many heartaches.

Reading through the Song of Songs recently, I was struck not as much by the poetry as the power of words. The romantic couple is intent on building their love. Everything they say to one another drips with passion. Then one evening the husband comes home late only to find the door locked. Knocking at her door, he begs her to let him in. This time she is a bit put out. It is late. She's already in bed and could care less about Prince Charming's predicament.

Later she feels differently and arises to open the door only to find him gone. Panicked, she goes and searches everywhere for him, until they are finally reunited in the next chapter.

The story is applicable for today. Often our harsh responses teach others that it is better to look elsewhere for love and understanding. When we realize our foolishness and come running, the friendship may have vanished. Sometimes a diligent pursuit is necessary if the relationship is ever to bloom again. Words hold power. What we say can bless our friendships or destroy them.

A Word to Husbands

Much of nurturing the marriage relationship seems to fall on the wife's shoulders. Statistically far more wives seek marriage counseling than husbands, and they are often the first to sense that the marriage is in trouble. Is this as it should be?

We can point back to creation and appreciate the relational differences that are part of God's design. Sin marred that unity of the first man and woman and made role definitions necessary. Yet we can also point to the cross where Christ died proving the equality of men and women, and tempering marriage roles with love. At Calvary, the husband's role changed. The Christian man is commanded to demonstrate sacrificial love for his wife. Christ's tender, unreserved love for the church is his model (Ephesians 5:23-29). Practically, this means the quality of the marriage relationship rests foremost on the husband's shoulders— not the wife's. It means, God expects him to lead the way in building the marriage relationship. Too often, the reverse is true.

Paul also speaks to Christian wives in this passage. He says: "Wives, submit to your husbands as to the Lord" (Ephesians 5:22). It sounds simple until you note the implied question behind the command: Husbands, how Christlike is your leadership in the home? The stark truth is this—that many wives would lovingly follow their husbands, if the husband would take Christlike responsibility for the marriage.

Both Lover and Friend

Developing a rewarding marital friendship is hard work. Without God's enabling, none of us could pull it off. Without His perspective, we might easily bypass the friendship marriage offers. There are few things as rewarding as a marriage in which intimacy and passion have been woven together. God wants to make this your experience as well. After healing the rift between them, the couple in Song of Songs summed up the potential of marriage in a classic statement. They said simply, "This is my lover, this my friend" (5:16). I hope you'll claim this as a goal for your marriage as well.

Making It Yours

1. Take a few minutes to remember some special moments you've spent with your spouse—a vacation, a date, your wedding day, etc. What do you enjoy most about that memory?

2. Would you consider your mate: a) a friend? b) a close friend? c) an enemy? d) my closest friend? e) an acquaintance?

   Why did you answer as you did? Would you like to change your answer? If so, how?

3. What keeps you from spending time with your mate?

4. List five things you enjoy doing.
   a.
   b.
   c.
   d.
   e.

   Now list five things your spouse enjoys doing.
   a.
   b.
   c.
   d.
   e.

Highlight any interests you share in common. Next, mark any of your spouse's interests that might have potential to become a shared interest. How might you transform some of these differences into bridges to positive memories?

5. Get honest with yourself. If a hidden camera were to record a week in your home, what would the record show?

6. Read Ephesians 4:25-32. As Christians, what qualities should characterize our relationships? Which of these areas presents the greatest personal challenge in your marriage?

7. Review the four perspectives given under "Reality Check." Which perspective gives you the greatest hope as you learn to love an imperfect mate?

8. Many couples don't consider counseling until it is nearly too late. Instead, let me urge you to think of counseling as personal pastoring. Going to an experienced, godly counselor will help you uncover wrong thinking that is hurting your marriage. Counseling also offers you a valuable source of accountability as you make changes. While not as effective, books written by experienced counselors can also yield fresh insights. Here are a few you might find helpful.

Love Is a Decision,
   by Gary Smalley with John Trent
Men Are from Mars, Women Are from Venus,
   by John Gray, Ph.D.
Rekindled,
   Pat and Jill Williams
His Need, Her Needs
   William F Harley, Jr.

Chapter 10

Closer Than a Brother

"Well, what do you think, Scott?" Cleve asked the young construction supervisor seated beside him. "Do you believe there is a God?" Outside the truck cab, the yellowed grasses along the roadside swayed and bent before an autumn breeze as Scott and Cleve drove past.

A moment of silence rested lightly between the two men. "I don't know," Scott confessed. "In college, I tried to figure that out. You know, I wanted to find the bottom line—what life was really all about. I tried different religions and failed to come to any conclusion. Eventually, I just decided not to worry about it and live for what I wanted." Scott paused. He didn't have much use for religious discussions or religious people. Cleve was a nice guy, but the subject was beginning to feel awkward. "I don't know if there is a God," Scott concluded the conversation. "But if there is, I'm sure He'll let me know."

Autumn days slipped by, the warm breezes of October were replaced by the gray, wintery gusts of November. Although Cleve and Scott continued to work together, the religious discussion shared a month earlier seemed forgotten. Indeed, Scott had other concerns on his mind. One day as they worked together, Scott shared his struggles with Cleve. Once again, Cleve began to tell Scott about Jesus. This time Scott was eager to listen.

The two men spent most of the day working and talking. For every statement Cleve made, Scott had an honest, searching question. That afternoon, as they returned from a job site, they stopped at a piece of property Scott had recently purchased. As he walked along a trail crossing the property, the pieces of the gospel finally made sense to him.

Today Scott recalls, "I never actually prayed to receive Christ. Instead, I consciously made a decision to surrender my life to Him. It is hard to explain. You see, Jesus seemed so real—so alive—at that moment in my life. I felt I would have had to ask Him to leave to lose that sense of His presence." It was an overwhelming and life-changing moment. Not only did Scott become a Christian that day, but the intimate friendship that God offers to mankind also became Scott's personal reality.

Proverbs 18:24 says, "A man of many companions may come to ruin, but there is a friend who sticks closer than a brother." God longs to be that special Friend. In fact, initiating an intimate friendship with mankind is the reason Christ came.

Divine Friendships Old and New

Moses was described as a friend of God. Abraham, David and others had similarly intimate relationships with God. Yet these rare Old Testament experiences pale in comparison with the friendship God offers us today.

In the Old Testament times God only revealed Himself to specific individuals. Moses is one example. While busy shepherding his flock one day, he saw a bush blazing with fire. Moses turned aside to get a better look, and that's when God spoke to him.

In their conversation God recruited Moses to lead the nation of Israel from their slavery in Egypt. When Moses was reluctant to obey, God provided Aaron as a teammate. Yet throughout the Exodus experience, it is Moses that God talked to and Moses that is later described as talking to God "as a man speaks with his friend" (Exodus 33:11).

So it would be with others God called and used. A little boy named Samuel would hear God's voice, while the aged priest Eli heard nothing (1 Samuel 3). God would appoint a cowardly farmer named Gideon to deliver Israel from the Midianites even though, by Gideon's own admission, there were others better suited for the job (Judges 6). Another time, God chose a simple shepherd boy over his seven older brothers to fill with His Spirit and anoint king of Israel (1 Samuel 16). Clearly, from Abraham through the prophet Malachi, God's offer of intimacy was selective. All were called to worship, but only a few were invited to draw near.

God was also innately unapproachable. Speaking to Moses from the burning bush, God warned Moses to keep his distance. Later, when Moses was invited into God's presence on Mount Horeb, strict boundaries were set up around the mountain. Anyone stepping over those boundaries was to be executed (Exodus 19:12, 13). And for all the "friendship" that existed between Moses and God, the most he ever saw of God was His back (33:18-23).

From the moment of His birth, Jesus was different. Heralded by angels and worshiped by curious shepherds, Jesus was God and yet man. He would claim the holy name of God (I AM) and yet respond to the common titles of Rabbi, Messiah, Emmanuel and Jesus, as well. While the Old Testament God held man off at a distance, Jesus brought him close. We read with wonder, as this God-man takes the time to touch a leper, goes out of His way to cast demons from crazed men and lovingly gathers children in His arms to bless them. Neither is Jesus' invitation to friendship selective. In Matthew 11:28-30, He invites everyone who is spiritually weary to find their soul's rest in Him.

Yet incredibly, the offer of divine friendship became even more personal when Jesus ascended to heaven. God's invitation to friendship is still open to all, but now is also sealed by the abiding presence of the Holy Spirit. Unlike the distant relationship that Moses had with God in ages past, we have been invited to a divine friendship of such intimacy that God lives within us! Instead of waiting to be called into God's presence or being limited by the physical realities of Jesus' schedule, we are granted continual access to God (Hebrews 4:16; 10:19-22). And while He is no less the mighty, holy I AM of Exodus, we are granted the tender privilege of calling Him *"Abba,* Father" (Romans 8:15). Granted, we can't see God now. God's agenda separates us from experiencing His friendship in a physical sense. When Jesus returns that will change. It is then that Christians will again feel His loving, personal touch as He wipes away our tears (Revelation 21:4).

There's Nothing Like It

Still, friendship with God is unique from all our other relationships. We touched on one aspect of this uniqueness when we observed that Christ offers us the ultimate intimate relationship through His indwelling Holy Spirit. Earthly friendships involve the interaction of two separate people. While friends share many things in common, their identities remain separate. Such is not the case for divine friendship.

In this relationship alone, God desires that we merge our identity with His. This is what Paul meant when he wrote: "For to me, to live is Christ and to die is gain" (Philippians 1:21). The moment you receive Christ, you begin the adventure of losing yourself in God's plan and identity. This is not to say you no longer have your own personality, talents and interests. We each have a unique place in God's plan. Yet, through Christ's influence, our essential character is gradually transformed until it becomes more like His.

Second, this is the only friendship where we are encouraged to worship our Friend. While many are tempted to make another person their idol, we are to worship Christ alone. Exalting another person to a place of equality with Christ leads only to heartache.

Third, no other friendship offers the same dividends as this divine invitation. While earthly friends can enrich our lives and influence us for good, only Christ offers the ability to transform our very nature. In doing so, this friendship also equips us to befriend others.

In her revealing book, *Choices Changes,* Joni Eareckson Tada tells of the day she went to have her wedding dress fitted. After arriving and having friends dress her in the gown, the fitting lady appeared. Nervously twisting her yellow tape measure in her fingers, she considered her wheelchair bound client. "'I am so sorry,'" she finally commented. "'I have never fitted someone like this.'" After which she refused to attempt taking the needed measurements.

At this point, the saleswoman returned. Grasping the awkwardness of the situation, she gently began working with the anxious tailor to complete the fitting. Later, as Joni prepared to leave, the saleswoman placed her hand on the armrest of Joni's wheelchair and said, "'You will look charming on your wedding day . . . I am a Christian, and I will be praying for you and your bridegroom that morning.' " (Eareckson Tada 1986, 245-247)

What led that saleswoman to befriend Joni at a time when she so desperately needed her intervention? Certainly it is possible to speculate a number of motivations. Yet I believe the woman's final testimony reveals the source of her compassion—her relationship with Jesus Christ.

First John 4:7 says: "Dear friends, let us love one another, for love comes from God. Everyone who loves has been born of God and knows God." Clearly, it is our friendship with God that enables us to truly befriend those around us. In fact, God intends our love for one another to extend even to costly personal sacrifice (1 John 4:10-11). This outpouring of love toward others is mute testimony to our friendship with Him. Our capacity for earthly friendship reflects the reality of God, and countless compassionate acts help complete His plan of love for the world (4:12). In fact, it is contradictory to speak of kindred spirit friendships apart from Jesus Christ. The source of true friendship begins in a personal relationship with Him.

Probably the most unique aspect of friendship with God is that it is a spiritual relationship. We don't see God. We can't touch Him or conduct an audible conversation. Instead, God communicates with us through our thoughts by means of His Holy Spirit. This is what Christians mean when they say, "That sermon really spoke to me," or "That verse has meant so much to me." In expressions like these, Christians attempt to explain how God personalizes a generic verse, sermon, etc., to apply to our specific need.

Our part of the conversation (prayer) is much less impressive. As needy friends we come asking His help or expressing our gratitude and praise in words we often find too limiting. Books abound on the subject of prayer and related forms like meditation. Yet the real killers of our relationship with God are attitudes, not techniques.

Busyness

Sweat beaded on her brow as she worked hard, kneading the bread with her strong, muscled hands. Pushing an errant strand of hair back with floured fingers, Martha hurried across the courtyard to check the fire smoldering within the oven. There was still so much to do. Why wasn't Mary helping her? The last Martha had glimpsed of her sister, Mary was sitting at Jesus' feet listening to His teaching. Certainly she should know that Martha would need her help. Why was she so long in coming?

Generations separate us, but I can understand Martha's happy anxiety as she works to prepare a nice meal for Jesus and His disciples. Entertaining special guests is fun, but it can also be lots of work. So I can empathize with Martha when she lashes out in exasperation at her sister, Mary.

"Lord," she protests, "don't you care that my sister has left me to do the work by myself? Tell her to help me!" (Luke 10:40).

I'm sure she never expected Jesus' answer. " 'Martha, Martha,' " the Lord answered, 'you are worried and upset about many things, but only one thing is needed. Mary has chosen what is better, and it will not be taken away from her' " (10:41-42).

Busyness probably robs God of more friendships than anything else. Like Martha, we often get so caught up in the rat race of life and service that time with Him vanishes completely. However, service that is not inspired by a loving relationship soon rings empty. Before long we find ourselves wondering why we are doing what we are. The meaning and joy of service evaporate as we move apart from quality time with God.

The lesson from Mary's example is not to forsake our calling or to exalt Christian service over secular employment as some mistakenly think. This moment in Mary's life highlights a truth basic to our friendship with God. Jesus asks simply that somehow we make time—quality time—with Him a priority. Serving God is no substitute for knowing Him.

Self-Sufficiency

"Just a minute, Vince," Michael said quickly as he paused his Nintendo game. "I need to pray!"

Five-year-old Vincent and I watched with amazement as Michael laid aside his control, folded his hands, bowed his head and began mouthing a silent, fervent prayer. A moment later, he opened his eyes and resumed his game with a brief explanation. "You need to pray, Vince, or you will never make it through the tough parts!"

I couldn't help laughing. Praying over a game of Nintendo was certainly something I'd never think to do. Still, my son's simple dependency on God pricked my own attitude of self-sufficiency. Too often I've left God in the shadows while claiming life's center stage in my own strength. Perhaps I could learn something from Michael's simple faith.

"Without faith it is impossible to please God," Hebrews 11:6 says. "Anyone who comes to him must believe that he exists and that he rewards those who earnestly seek him." I remember memorizing this passage, but learning to live by it has been much harder. Yet faith is basic to a relationship with God. We neither please Him nor relate to Him without it.

Sometime after Michael's Nintendo prayer, I asked him what he said to God in those moments. "Oh," he responded. "I said, 'but the learning'God, you know this is a really tough part and I can't make it through without your help. Please help me.' "

"Did God help you?" I queried further.

"Oh, yes," Michael said, in his little boy, matter-of-fact faith. "God always helps me."

Perhaps this is what Jesus meant when He said that the kingdom of heaven belongs to children (Luke 18:16, 17). I can't help but wonder if perhaps Jesus enjoys a warmer friendship with my six-year-old than with his self-sufficient mother. How about you?

Hardness

The 20th century saw the widespread application of a remarkable medical breakthrough — immunization. The concept was to inject the patient with a weak strain of a certain virus. If all went well, this would trigger the body's immune system to develop white blood cells to combat the illness, resulting in a permanent defense against it.

For most people, physical immunization provides invaluable protection. But there is another kind of immunization that isn't positive. I'm referring to the spiritual barriers we often raise against God Himself.

In Hebrews 3 the author warns Christians of the danger of becoming immunized against God. He writes: "Encourage one another daily, as long as it is called Today, so that none of you may be hardened by sin's deceitfulness" (3:13). It is so easy to become calloused to the prompting of God's Spirit. Apathy quickly quenches moral outrage. Greed robs compassion of her gifts. Bitterness holds out over forgiveness. In time, selfishness can dethrone Christ as Lord of our lives. Outwardly, we may appear the same —church attenders, morally upright, etc.—but a spiritual chill has wound itself around our hearts. When the Holy Spirit speaks to us, we refuse to listen. Like the Christians Paul describes in Second Timothy 3:5, we have a form of godliness, but have denied its power.

To have an intimate friendship with God, we must be willing to listen and respond to His leading. I've met many Christians who have walked with God to a point of conviction and then stopped.

Frank was such a person. He professed to know Christ, lived an honest life, even held a position of leadership in his local church. But as I got to know Frank outside of church, I realized I'd met up with a spiritual chameleon. Like the notorious lizard, Frank changed his behavior to match his environment. He reflected Christian actions and convictions in church and the behavior of the world the rest of the week. Frank wasn't a bad man, just spiritually empty. Whenever conversation turned to spiritual issues, there was little or no response.

Was Frank a Christian? He certainly professed to being one. If so, he was a Christian that was no longer pursuing his friendship with Jesus Christ. Somewhere along the way he had hardened his heart against the Holy Spirit. Unless Frank repents and actively renews his friendship with Christ, he'll be left with nothing more than his game of spiritual chameleon. Quite simply, it is impossible to have fellowship with Christ without recognizing His lordship.

Compromise

Compromising describes the effort to find middle ground between two extremes. Starting in childhood, we practice compromising until hopefully we become adept at knowing when and how to use it in solving adult conflicts. In human relationships, the ability to compromise when necessary is a powerful and positive skill.

It is only in friendship with God that compromise becomes a moral issue. In eternity God has mapped out a perfect plan for our lives. Through friendship with Him, God desires to lead us into that plan. It is not that our perspectives, feelings and desires aren't important. God has already taken them into account. But in this friendship there is no room for compromise, no middle ground between our wants and God's plan. When we try to force a compromise between the two, we are sinning.

The Christians in Laodicea were notorious for their ability to compromise. They weren't a liberal church exactly. Slip into a pew there any Sunday morning and you'd hear a solid sermon. Instead, I imagine, they were a respectable middle-of-the-road kind of church. They filled a place in the community, never made any waves nor caused any scandals. In fact, they were quite comfortable in their relationship with God.

God felt differently, however.

> "These are the words of the Amen, the faithful and true witness, the ruler of God's creation. I know your deeds, that you are neither cold nor hot. I wish you were either one or the other! So, because you are lukewarm—neither hot nor cold—I am about to spit you out of my mouth" (Revelation 3:14-16).

I don't know what it is like where you live, but coffee mania has washed over the Pacific Northwest. Everywhere I look there are espresso stands, coffee shops, coffee grinders, etc. The craze even has its own lingo. You can choose from caffé mocha, caffé latte, cappuccino, iced coffee and a limitless variety of blends. I've noticed, however, that no one sells lukewarm coffee. Probably because lukewarm coffee, no matter what blend or mix, is downright awful. It doesn't cool you down, and it won't heat you up. Instead it tastes old and flat. In fact, drinking lukewarm coffee is almost worse than having none at all. I don't know if God's a coffee drinker, but the analogy echoes His words to the Christians in Laodicea. You are either for God or against Him. When we try to strike a compromise between His will and ours, the result, like lukewarm coffee, is sickening.

Bill and Barb were convinced God was calling them into full-time Christian work. After working out some details, they moved to a Bible school where Bill could get the training he'd need. They never saw graduation day. The financial and time pressures of Bill's schooling and Barb's employment wore their commitment thin. Instead, after a year or so, they left. Bill took a factory job and they settled down in a small town to raise their family. Although they attended church regularly, their involvement was marginal. When I met Bill and Barb, the decision to leave college was decades behind them. Yet the guilt and regrets over their decision remained fresh in their memories, clearly hindering them from enjoying a growing relationship with God.

What's the solution for those of us like Bill and Barb? We all occasionally attempt compromise with God. How can we keep our friendship with God refreshingly alive? The cure for the Christians in Laodicea is the same for us as well: "Those whom I love I rebuke and discipline. So be earnest, and repent" (Revelation 3:19). Bill and Barb need not have lived with stunted Christian experiences. True repentance would have fanned alive the spark of the Holy Spirit within them. Instead, they chose the lukewarm path of compromise. They had their creed, their church involvement and all the doctrinal answers they would ever need. What they sacrificed was vitality in their relationship with Christ.

Sin

Sin ruptures our relationship with Christ like nothing else. In Genesis, mankind's original fall from grace resulted in a spiritual alienation from God that only Christ's death on Calvary could remedy. If we refuse to accept God's provision for sin through Christ's death, we remain God's enemies—not His friends (see Colossians 1:21-22). But sin continues to be a problem even for those who have received Christ's offer of forgiveness. It is a problem because sin, whether we are an atheist or a Christian, always alienates us from God.

Picture in your mind a high mountain lake. By early fall a fine sheet of ice stretches across the surface. The ice is so thin it's almost invisible. By mid-winter, however, the ice on the lake will be a thick, crusty coating, hiding the life-giving water below it. Sin is similar to the ice coating this lake. Our friendship with Christ offers us vitality, purpose, forgiveness and strength—qualities basic to living a full and meaningful life. When we sin, by living in opposition to God's plan, a silent, invisible barrier of guilt interrupts our fellowship. God continues to offer us a rewarding friendship with Him. It is our rebellion that makes us unable to repent and break through to relate to God afresh. Over time sin can become a lifestyle. We can callous our hearts to guilt, like so many new layers of ice on a winter lake. Sadly, some resist God's friendship until eventually it is nearly impossible for them to break through the layers of rebellion to all that He longs to give.

Closer Than a Brother

How would you describe your friendship with God? Are you experiencing the warm, vital, intimate relationship that Christ came to give, or something far less personal? A huge stained glass picture of Christ knocking on the door of a cottage graced the center window of the church I attended as a child. In time, I came to understand the Scripture that inspired the artist: "Here I am! I stand at the door and knock. If anyone hears my voice and opens the door, I will come in and eat with him, and he with me" (Revelation 3:20).

I learned that Jesus knocks at the life of every man and woman, boy and girl, waiting to be invited in. For those that welcome Him, He enters casting His forgiveness over their sins, transforming their lives by His influence. It wasn't until later that I realized this passage is actually addressed to those who have already trusted in Christ for salvation. Why then is Christ pictured outside the lives of Christians? Could it be that attitudes like those we've been considering forced Him from His place of welcome?

On March 28, 1978, I finally answered Christ's knocking at my life's door. I was desperate for forgiveness and meaning in life. In a simple prayer of welcome, I threw my heart's door open. Christ entered, giving me so much more than I ever dreamed possible. Not only was I offered the forgiveness and meaning I longed for, but I also found a comforting, guiding Friend as well.

Today my friendship with Christ is still the rich adventure it has ever been. Friendship with Christ has resulted not just in life—but in a quality life experience. Under His influence I've faced challenges I would otherwise never have attempted. It has meant experiencing comfort in the midst of heartache, sensing His design even in periods of transitional loneliness. Repeatedly, I've been overwhelmed by His abundant generosity and faithfulness. In areas of my life needing change, He's helped me exercise self-control. And when I'm confused by life's problems, I can come to Him with my questions. The answers I need don't necessarily drop out of heaven, but guidance always comes. Oh, there are times when I fall back into my old patterns of self-sufficiency and rebellion. But I'm learning to rely on His faithful, loving friendship more all the time.

Few ties are stronger than those that connect family members. Yet there is a Friend that is closer than any brother. His name is Jesus. I hope you know Him and keep on getting to know Him. Intimate friendship issues from the heart of God. And as we'll see, knowing Him as a friend equips us to warmly befriend the world around us.

Making It Yours

1. What does your personal relationship with Christ mean to you? Would you describe your relationship with Him as an intimate friendship?

2. In what ways does your friendship with God differ from your other friendships?

3. "Books abound on the subject of prayer and related forms, like meditation. Yet the real killers of our relationship with God are attitudes not techniques." Do you agree or disagree with this statement? Explain your reasoning.

4. Read Luke 10:38-42. What did Martha need to learn about her friendship with Jesus?

How can you apply her experience to your own life?

5. What effect does sin have on our relationship with Christ? (Psalm 66:18; Isaiah 59:1,2)

6. Read and then rewrite James 4:4 in your own words.

_____

_____

_____

When your will and God's will are at odds, is it possible to strike a compromise and maintain the integrity of your friendship?

7. Explain the difference between self-initiative and self-sufficiency.

Read Philippians 3:7-10. Paul's previous self-sufficient attitude kept him from experiencing at least two spiritual benefits. What are they?

_____(3:9)

_____(3:10)

8. Are the attitudes discussed in this chapter (busyness, self-sufficiency, hardness of heart, spiritual compromises and sin) really different attitudes, or merely variations of sin itself? Which attitude (if any) currently hinders your relationship with Christ? What is the biblical solution? (Revelation 3:19, 20)

9. According to Revelation 3:20, where is Jesus now in relationship to your life—outside or inside? If Christ is inside your life, take a few minutes and write how and when He came into your life. Include enough details to bring out the story it is. When you are finished, make a copy as a future legacy for your family. If you are using this book in a group study, you might enjoy reading or telling your testimonies to one another. If you've never invited Christ into your life, talk to a Christian friend, your Bible study leader or pastor. They will be eager to explain how to invite Christ into your life and help you understand what this decision means.

Chapter 11

What Is Christian Love Anyway?

I steered our white Toyota onto the interstate behind the Ryder rental truck my husband was driving. It was 4 a.m. on an April morning outside of Bozeman, Montana—a stop en route in the move to our new ministry in Omaha, Nebraska. Sierra dozed in the seat next to me. Our sedated cat mewed pathetically from its cage among the suitcases on the back seat. I slipped a cassette into my tape player and slid the headphones in place.

It was raining hard now. The wipers swept back and forth across the windshield fighting the wind and rain outside. But nothing could ease the emotional storm inside my heart. And there was no one to wipe my tears as I followed Scott across the darkened prairies of eastern Montana. Long ago I'd promised to follow the Lord wherever He would lead me. How could I have known that loving Him would also mean loving others so deeply?

Christian love and Christian friendship are ultimately bound together. Indeed, Christian friendship springs from Christian love. But what is Christian love? Is it emotion, like the heartache I experienced that morning outside of Bozeman? Or is Christian love something more aloof? Is love something we do, say or accept by faith? What did Paul mean when he listed love as one of the things that will last for eternity? (see 1 Corinthians 13:13). And if believers are commanded to love each other, how do we begin?

Love really begins with God. He is our Example and our Source. First John 4:8 says simply, "God is love." Love is an elusive concept to explain partly because Christian love is so foreign to us. Love issues from the nature of God Himself. I doubt if we will ever understand it perfectly on this side of eternity. It is clear, however, that Christian love is characterized by at least four things.

1. It's Personal: Love Knows

The first of these is that Christian love is personal. We live in a world that is increasingly impersonal. We talk about making love, loving a show or experiencing that special "chemistry" between two people. We sign our letters with the word "Love," and say "I love you" to relatives we see once a year. Love is definitely an overworked term.

In contrast, Christian love is personal particularly when it comes to marriage. Throughout the Bible, love and relationship are linked together. In Genesis 4:1 the Bible says, "Adam lay with his wife Eve." We may easily brush past this verse, but the Hebrew word translated "lay" is significant. The word is actually *yada* and describes a special, intimate knowledge. It is clear that Adam and Eve's sexual union was the result of a deeper emotional relationship. Theirs was not the passion of mere lust but was sexual experience that had grown out of their intimate knowledge of one another. From the beginning, knowledge preceded love.

But the use of *yada* is not limited to describing sex. The word appears again in Deuteronomy 34:10. This time *yada* describes the intimate relational knowledge that God had of Moses: "Since then, no prophet has risen in Israel like Moses, whom the LORD knew [*yada*] face to face."

Moses is described as God's friend. "The LORD would speak to Moses face to face, as a man speaks with his friend" (Exodus 33:11). It was not a physical relationship. Their relationship was solely spiritual. But it was a deep, intimate love relationship all the same. And again *yada* preceded love.

Yada is replaced in the New Testament with three similar Greek words: *oida, ginosko* and *epiginosko*. All three words have the concept of knowledge in common. Their differences concern the depth of the knowledge implied.

Oida means knowledge that springs from a close relationship. It is intimate knowledge that might come from living with someone and might be considered a New Testament counterpart to *yada*. For example, *oida* describes God's fatherly love in Matthew 7:11. Jesus asked: "If you, then, though you are evil, know [*oida*] how to give good gifts to your children, how much more will your Father in heaven give good gifts to those who ask him!" Jesus was pointing out that God's knowledge of our needs is even greater than the knowledge and compassion that human fathers have toward their children. God's knowledge, like that of most human fathers, is knowledge tempered with love.

Ginosko means an intellectual understanding. The English language takes its words for knowledge from this family of Greek words. Further, the Jews believed that what was known should be applied to life. So in the Jewish context, knowledge also led to change. *Ginosko* is the Greek word used in First Corinthians 13:12 when Paul wrote: "I know in part; then I shall know fully. . . ." Here Paul admitted that his current understanding of spiritual things was incomplete. He also anticipated that someday that would not be the case. When that day came, full knowledge would replace incomplete knowledge with Paul's life fully transformed according to God's intention.

Then Paul notes another kind of knowledge. *Epiginosko* is the word translated as known in "even as I am fully known" (13:12). *Epiginosko* describes a full and thorough kind of knowing. This is the kind of knowledge that God has of us. He knows us completely.

This is not to say that one word for knowledge is superior to another. It does however, highlight the link between knowing and loving. Whether it is friendship within marriage, between friends and family or more distant alliances, Christian love is based first on relationship.

Christian love is not impersonal. The love described in First Corinthians 13 is *agape*—the same unconditional love that God has toward all mankind. However, unconditional love is not impersonal love. We live in a fast-paced world. Everything seems marketed on the basis of personal convenience. But when it comes to relationships, God calls us to something deeper. Christian love asks us to slow down, to set our personal agendas aside and get to know one another. For it is only as we know one another that we can truly love as Christ would have us love.

It was a hot day. Jesus was tired, hungry and thirsty as He and His disciples approached the town of Sychar. No doubt the disciples wondered why He had chosen this route to Galilee. Most devout Jews took another path that bypassed the despised Samaritans completely. Now they were forced to stop here. Leaving Jesus at the well, the disciples went on into town to find something to eat.

While Jesus was resting there, someone came to draw water. She was alone, a woman and a Samaritan—socially acceptable reasons for Jesus to ignore her. Beginning with a request for water, Jesus talked with this lonely woman. By the end of their conversation, He had led her to faith in Him. The woman's conversion rippled through the community. Instead of simply stopping for lunch, Jesus stayed in Sychar an extra two days, with the result that many placed their faith in Him (see John 4:41-42).

It was love that made Jesus stop and initiate a conversation with a woman no one else would talk to. He could have declared His deity to her from the start. Why ask questions about her past anyway? She probably didn't want to talk about it. Yet it was love that uncovered her need, if not to Christ, then most certainly to herself.

Jesus took the time to relate, to know, to be personal. In the end, it became the conduit for a new beginning. Encounters like this happened repeatedly in Jesus' ministry. He was a man with a mission, but the fact that He took time for people showed that Jesus was also a man of compassion.

2. It's Practical: Love Acts

Not only is love personal, but true love is demonstrative. Love proves itself in action. One friend noted, "It is hard to talk about love apart from what love does. It's what love does that IS love." How right he is. We are reminded in First John 3:16, "This is how we know what love is: Jesus Christ laid down his life for us. And we ought to lay down our lives for our brothers." What does this mean? The answer is reflected in the life of Jesus.

Walking was the primary means of transportation in Christ's day. The country roads were dusty. Within the cities, the streets smelled of refuse and animal dung. It's not surprising then that the practice of having a servant wash guests' feet was a Palestinian expression of hospitality. It's equally understandable that it was usually performed by the lowliest servant in the household.

But no such servant was available the night Jesus and His disciples gathered to eat their final meal together. Jesus could have asked the youngest disciple to wash their feet. He didn't. Jesus knew Judas would soon betray Him. He could have asked Judas to wash their feet that evening. Or perhaps the service could have been laid aside this one time. After all, the account in the book of John indicates they were already eating supper. Would it matter to do without this gesture? It mattered to Christ because this was an opportunity to actively love one another.

Instead of overlooking the issue, Jesus took the place of a servant. Quietly He left the table and laid aside His outer robe. Then, with towel and basin in hand, He knelt beside each disciple, gently washing their dirty, tired feet. When He resumed His place at the table, Jesus taught them a powerful lesson in love:

> I, your Lord and Teacher, have washed your feet, you also should wash one another's feet. I have set you an example that you should do as I have done for you. (1 John 13:14-15)

This example is mirrored in the verse when it says: "This is how we know what love is: Jesus Christ laid down his life for us." (3:16) The Greek expression for "laid down his life" in this verse is identical to the description of Jesus laying aside His outer robe in the Upper Room that evening. The thought here is that both in His death, as well as in the Upper Room that evening, Christ actively set aside His rights to minister to those in need. These are only two among many practical ways that Christ demonstrated His love for others. Christ calls us to follow His example. In practical acts of sacrifice as lowly as washing feet, or as lofty as surrendering our lives, Christian love calls us to lay aside our rights and practically love another.

Ruth shivered and blew on her numb fingers as she walked toward the checkout stand. It was December—the Christmas season. But there was little cheer in her heart. She was still reeling from the devastating blow of divorce. Her marriage had unraveled quickly over the past few years. Ruth's ex-husband, Mike, had seemed unable to find steady work. Finally she took a job bagging groceries at a local market. It was steady work, but didn't pay enough to support them all—herself, their three-year-old child and Mike. Eventually, Ruth gave Mike an ultimatum: get a job or get out. Mike chose to leave. The divorce soon followed. Now Ruth faced the future—and Christmas—alone.

She didn't think about all that now. Instead her red, aching hands moved quickly to bag the groceries in front of her. "Can I help you out?" she asked mechanically, hardly focusing on the graying woman at the counter.

"Yes, that would be nice. Thank you," responded the woman. Ruth fell into step behind the customer, and they slipped through the automatic doors into the blustery cold waiting outside.

The woman made small talk as they walked across the parking lot. "It's cold, today. You must be freezing!"

"I'm used to it," Ruth responded, trying to stifle a shiver and move as quickly as possible.

"You should wear a hat and some gloves," the older woman persisted.

Ruth hefted the last sack from the cart to the car. "I don't have any," Ruth said. "I manage. Have a nice day."

The woman climbed into her car. By the time Ruth reached the store entrance, the woman's blue sedan was pulling out onto the boulevard.

Snow was falling in big powdery white flakes. The encounter slipped from Ruth's mind.

Later, as the afternoon ebbed toward evening, Ruth heard a familiar voice. It was the same woman she had waited on that morning. Only this time she had a package in her hands.

"Here," she said holding out the brightly wrapped parcel. "This is for you. I made them to give to someone else. But I felt you needed them more. Merry Christmas!"

Ruth was numb with surprise. Slowly she unwrapped the soft parcel. Inside were a pair of hand knitted mittens. Tears rolled down Ruth's cheeks. It wasn't the gift that mattered so much as the act. Someone cared. Someone really cared. Ruth told me later, "That day made Christmas for me. Nothing else mattered after that."

Love is action. That woman could have talked to Ruth about God's love, but it was what she did that spoke volumes. When we act on an opportunity to share or sacrifice a little for someone else, we are loving as Christ did. It may be as simple as a note or phone call, or something far more costly. Ultimately, it's our actions that speak the loudest.

3. It's Strong: Love Feels

Love is a strong emotion. Anyone who has been "in love" can tell you that. They may have said or done things that they've never said or done since. Should this passionate nature of love be expected of Christian brotherly love as well? When First John 4:8 describes God as love itself, does this mean that He is a sugarcoated deity, intent on giving us only good emotional experiences?

To answer these questions we must begin with a look at God, the Author of love. God has always been passionate. In Genesis 1 the expression "it was good" is repeated seven times. The expression means to cry out. Literally, God was so excited about His creation that His words rang throughout the universe as He gave voice to His pleasure not once, but seven times! Yes, God is passionate.

When Adam sinned, God's love turned to anger. God didn't hate man. He hated the sin that separated them. Adam and Eve left Eden forever because the loving relationship with God that existed previously would never be the same. Sin had barred the way.

The Old Testament reads like an ancient soap opera of God's love extended, received and repulsed. In the generations to come, God continually sought to draw man to Himself. Some of them (Enoch, Noah, Abraham, etc.) responded to God, but most did not. In time, God raised up the nation of Israel to illustrate His passionate nature. Israel continually wandered from God, even so far as to embrace idolatry. God sent hardship to turn Israel back to Him. They came, but they wouldn't stay. He sent prophets to warn them of the consequences of sin. Eventually, God allowed them to suffer in exile for 70 years. When they returned, they worshiped God outwardly but their hearts were hard as stone. Finally, God called the prophet Hosea to bear unfaithfulness in his own marriage in order to illustrate God's love for Israel. The divine heartache is undeniable. In Chapter 11, Hosea summed up God's experience:

> When Israel was a child, I loved him, and out of Egypt I called my son . . . It was I who taught Ephraim to walk, taking them by the arms; but they did not realize it was I who healed them. I led them with cords of human kindness, with ties of love; I lifted the yoke from their neck and bent down to feed them. . . . My people are determined to turn from me. . . . How can I give you up, Ephraim? How can I hand you over, Israel? . . . My heart is changed within me; all my compassion is aroused. (11:1, 3, 4, 7, 8)

Such a love is beyond human comprehension. No earthly illustration can fully explain God's passion for mankind. Yet I better understood God's love after an experience in my own family. It was a bright Sunday morning. I stepped out the back door of the parsonage, as I'd done countless times, and walked the short 50-foot commute to the church building. My two-year-old, Sierra, walked beside me. I usually held her hand, but that day my arms were filled with other things. As I awkwardly shuffled my load to open the side door to the church, Sierra headed toward the front of the building. The front entrance was flanked by a long porch. Sierra enjoyed playing there. *She's probably headed out front to play,* I thought to myself. *I'll set my things down, and collect her in a moment.*

A few minutes later, I made my way to the front entrance. "Sierra," I called loudly. "It's time to come in." There was no answer. I walked to the front of the church. Sierra was nowhere in sight. Quickly I retraced my steps to the parsonage. *Maybe she went back home for something,* I thought, irritation and worry beginning to eat at the edges of my composure. "Sierra," I called more forcefully. "Come here! It's time for church!" But still there was no response and I became worried.

I called my husband, and we began to search together. "Where could she have gone?" I asked half in panic. "I only left her for a minute!" We checked an empty building across the street, peered anxiously down steep cellar steps. There was no sign of her anywhere! Meanwhile, my fear was taking giant leaps of imagination in my mind. What could have happened to my little girl? My heart was racing to keep pace with my emotions.

Finally Scott drove around the block. That's when he spotted Sierra. As Scott turned the corner, he saw Betty and Sierra walking hand-in-hand back up the street. Betty who lived at the end of our block made some of the best chocolate chip cookies I've ever tasted. Sierra and I stopped almost daily to visit with Betty and help her with errands. Often we enjoyed some of her delicious cookies. That Sunday morning, Sierra decided one of those cookies would taste pretty good. Instead of playing on the front porch of the church, she had calmly walked to Betty's for a cookie.

Never has my little girl seemed so precious as she did in those anxious moments before we were reunited. I hugged her tight, tears coursing down my cheeks. Then I gave her a lecture she'd never forget!

As I held Sierra that morning, I knew the passion of a mother's love. But I also caught a glimpse of God the Father's love for His own. My daughter was lost for only a few minutes. Apart from Christ, man is separated from his Creator for all eternity. We can only imagine God's pain. The prophet Isaiah captures it best:

> Can a mother forget the baby at her breast
> and have no compassion on the child
> she has borne?
> Though she may forget,
> I will not forget you!
> See, I have engraved you on the palms

of my hands;
  your walls are ever before me.
    (Isaiah 49:15-16)

Is God's love passionate? Without question! Likewise, Christians are to love passionately as well. But what is passionate Christian love? Forgiveness is the wellspring of passion. Because Christian love is subject to Christ's lordship, the focus is never what I want, but what God wants. The emotional experience of Christian love overflows from living in obedience to Christ. And forgiveness is an essential part of obedience.

Christian love doesn't condemn hurt and anger or try to whitewash injustice. It does, however, mandate that we bring our passions under Christ's direction, surrender revenge to God and begin actively loving our brother. To do this is contrary to our natural passions. And this is where the passions of the world and the passions of God separate. The key is in the cross. God's love enables us to love when we feel least able to.

Peter admonished Christians to "love one another deeply, from the heart" (1 Peter 1:22b). Other translations use the word fervently to describe the type of love we should have for one another. Thankfully, God doesn't expect us to generate those feelings ourselves. Peter clearly indicates that such love—passionate Christian love—is predi-

cated on cleansing our souls before the cross
and living in faithful obedience to Christ. Dr.
Dan Allender writes:

> "Love is dependent on forgiveness. . . .
> The extent to which someone truly loves
> will be positively correlated to the degree
> the person is stunned and silenced by the
> wonder that his huge debt has been can-
> celed" (*Bold Love* 1992, 43).

What keeps you from passionately loving your
Christian brother or sister? Are their sins any
harder to forgive than yours? The old expression,
"There, but for the grace of God, go I," serves as a
reminder to all who ask the question. Passionate
Christian love begins at the cross.

4. It's Spiritual: Love Endures

With our increasingly mobile lifestyle, maintaining enduring friendships has become a
challenge. But Christian love has a relational
foundation that endures. Ultimately everything
else in life will end. It is only the personal, sacrificial bond between believers that we will take
with us into eternity. In its purest form, we
might call this bond a type of friendship which
transcends any superficial or sexual aspects of a
relationship.

Heaven will be a glorious experience. It is
there that Christian friendship will reach its
fullest expression. Can you imagine having all
eternity to worship God and fellowship to-

gether? Friends who have been parted by death will be reunited. Gone will be the weight of sin and temptation. There will be no more arguments or misunderstandings. Difficult goodbyes will be but a distant memory. Instead, time with friends will be endless. Selfish interests that marred our experience on earth will be displaced by a compelling desire to do God's will. Friendship may begin here, but heaven is its ultimate destiny.

And it is this eternal aspect of Christian love that yields such hope. Life is transitional. Time is our enemy. Busy schedules, moves, misunderstandings and death interrupt the ongoing intimacy we all seek. Yet because of Christ, Christian friends can look beyond today. Sheldon Vanauken sums up the enduring nature of Christian love as he describes parting from his close friend, C.S. Lewis:

> On that last day I met C. S. Lewis at the Eastgate for lunch. . . . Lewis said that he hoped Davy and I would be coming back to England soon, for we mustn't get out of touch. "At all events," he said with a cheerful grin, "we'll certainly meet again, here—or there." Then it was time to go. . . When we emerged on to the busy High with the traffic streaming past, we shook hands, and he said: "I shan't say goodbye. We'll meet again." Then he plunged into the traffic. I stood there watching him.

When he reached the pavement on the other side, he turned round as though he knew somehow that I would still be standing there. . . . Then he raised his voice in a great roar that easily overcame the noise of the cars and buses. . . . "Besides," he bellowed with a great grin, "Christians NEVER say goodbye!" (Vanauken 1977, 123)

Summary

So what is Christian love? It's taking the time and effort to be personal enough to get to know one another. As we know one another, God's love also empowers us to serve one another. This service may begin as an act of obedience to the Holy Spirit's prompting, but where Christian love is operative, emotions soon follow. In fact, the more we reflect on Christ's immense personal love for us, the more our own hearts will warm to those around us. Christian love is really a natural overflow of our personal love relationship with Christ. This is why C.S. Lewis described friendship as the love most like God's; it is wholly centered on the other. While many aspects of our relationships will end at the grave, Christian love—Christian friendship—extends into eternity. There we will understand what we can only glimpse now. As Paul wrote: "Now I know in part; then I shall know fully, even as I am fully known. And now these three remain: faith, hope and love. But the greatest of these is love" (1 Corinthians 13:12-13).

Making It Yours

1. Read First Corinthians 13 and list the verses from this chapter that highlight the four aspects of Christian love given below.

A. Christian love is *personal*. It is always preceded by knowledge.
(Reference)

B. Christian love is *practical*. It takes steps to help when help is needed.
(Reference)

C. Christian love is *emotional* but always tempered by godly self-control.
(Reference)

D. Christian love is first a *spiritual relationship* and therefore *eternal*.
(Reference)

2. Read and compare Jesus' visits with the man at Bethesda (John 5:1-17) and the Samaritan woman (4:1-26). How is listening to another part of loving that person? How should this affect the way we minister to others?

3. The day Christ died He prayed, "Father, forgive them, for they do not know what they are doing" (Luke 23:34). The word Je-

sus used for "know" *(oida)* means an intimate understanding. Jesus extended His
forgiveness because He realized the crowd
didn't fully understand who they were exe-
cuting.

Is there someone who has hurt you that
may not fully understand the consequences
of their actions? How could you apply
Christ's example to this relationship in your
life?

4. Read First John 4:16-18. Does this passage
   mean that we should respond to every
   Christian with a need? How does the "personal" dimension to Christian love help us
   practically love one another?

5. Why could C.S. Lewis shout to his friend,
   Sheldon: "Christians NEVER say goodbye!"?

Chapter 12

Jonathan and David:
The Power of Friendship

In 1885 an American novel about friendship
rolled off the press entitled *The Adventures of
Huckleberry Finn*. It quickly became an enduring
favorite. In the story, two unlikely friends, a
black slave named Jim, and a poor white boy,
named Huck Finn, team up to escape slavery
and abuse. Their joint efforts grow into more
than simple adventures. In the process of dodg-
ing steamboats, bounty hunters and frauds, Jim
and Huck forge a powerful friendship. It is a relationship that repeatedly tests Huck's loyalty
and softens Jim's distrust of "white folk." By
the end of the tale, both have changed. They
are free from their pasts, but their friendship
has also overstepped the boundaries of prejudice. Friendship has won the day.

The story remains a favorite, largely due to
its innocent, adventurous appeal. But the story
also hits a relational cord within us. Secretly we

all desire friendships that will transform us into better human beings. In our hearts (and in our fiction) we know that few things rival the creative power of friendship. Those whom we associate with inevitably shape our characters and influence our futures. It is a power than can be used for either good or bad.

Solitary independence isn't the scriptural ideal either. A God-and-I-versus-the-world attitude is not supported in the Bible. Instead God has placed us in a community of believers—the church. Within the church, God desires Christians to nurture deep, intimate friendships. He does so because of the creative, life-molding power of our friendships. Under His influence, godly friends are capable of helping us become all that God intends. They are personalized channels for His power and grace. Considered in this light, friendship is an awesome privilege and an equally serious responsibility. Fun, food and fellowship may all be part of time spent with friends, but God desires that our impact reach deeper.

Perhaps this is why so much attention is given in the Scriptures to the remarkable friendship between Jonathan and David. Through all of time, no other friendship has reflected God's presence quite as well.

Jonathan and David

The first recorded meeting of Jonathan and David was in the Valley of Elah following

David's miraculous victory over the Philistine champion, Goliath (see 1 Samuel 17). The two men may have met earlier. In chapter 16 we learn that David had previously spent time in Saul's courts as a musician and as Saul's armor bearer. Perhaps it was during those days that Jonathan's and David's friendship began. Regardless, following David's victory the Bible says that the two men became close friends. Jonathan loved David deeply and selflessly. The Bible says, "Jonathan became one in spirit with David, and he loved him as himself" (18:1). In fact, Jonathan removed his royal robe and armor and gave them to David. It was a sacrificial gift that carried deep meaning.

King Saul recognized military talent when he saw it. David's performance against Goliath convinced him that here was a young man with promise. In response to Saul's offer, David left shepherding behind him and became a soldier. Success followed every mission assigned him and he rose quickly to a place of leadership in Saul's army.

But while Jonathan's and David's friendship continued to deepen, Saul's love for David soured. Because of Saul's disobedience in an earlier clash with the Philistines, God had decreed that Jonathan would never follow his father to the throne. Samuel told Saul, "The Lord has sought out a man after his own heart and appointed him leader of his people, because

you have not kept the Lord's command"
(13:14).

Instead of responding to the message in repentance, Saul hardened his heart. From that
day forward, he was ever looking for his
dreaded successor. Now as Saul watched
David's success, he was reminded that God's
blessing no longer rested upon his life. Then
came the day the women sang in the streets
to welcome King Saul and his troops returning home from battle. "Saul has slain his thousands, and David his tens of thousands"
(18:7), they sang to the melody of lutes and
percussion of tambourines. The song seemed
to justify Saul's suspicions. Immediately the
bitterness in his soul calcified into a murderous mixture of envy, fear and hate. Saul rumi-
nated, "They have credited David with tens
of thousands, . . . but me with only thousands. What more can he get but the kingdom?" (18:8).

In spite of the growing tension between
David and King Saul, David's friendship with
Jonathan held true. When Saul ordered his servants to kill David, Jonathan quickly interceded
for his friend. "Let not the king do wrong to his
servant David," Jonathan protested. "He has
not wronged you, and what he has done has
benefited you greatly. . . . Why then would you
do wrong to an innocent man like David by
killing him for no reason?" (19:4-5). Although
increasingly   paranoid,   Saul   listened   to

Jonathan's appeal. David was reinstated in the palace as before.

The reprieve from Saul's suspicions was only temporary, however. Before long, Saul again gave orders for David's murder. This time David narrowly escaped as he fled. Eventually David was able to meet secretly with Jonathan, who had been unaware of his father's renewed aggression. David told his friend,

> "Your father knows very well that I have found favor in your eyes, and he has said to himself, 'Jonathan must not know this or he will be grieved.' Yet as surely as the LORD lives and as you live, there is only a step between me and death."

> Jonathan said to David, "Whatever you want me to do, I'll do for you." (20:3-4)

So it was planned that Jonathan would intercede once again on David's behalf. They renewed the covenant he and David shared in the Valley of Elah so long ago. Jonathan said to David,

> "May the LORD be with you as he has been with my father. But show me unfailing kindness like that of the LORD as long as I live, so that I may not be killed, and do not ever cut off your kindness from my family—not even when the LORD has cut off every one of David's enemies from the face of the earth." (20:13-15)

The two men arranged another meeting when Jonathan would share the results of his efforts for peace. This time, however, Jonathan's appeals were rejected. Saul raged at his son for defending David. When Jonathan pressed the issue, Saul hurled a spear at Jonathan in an attempt to kill him as well.

Later, meeting secretly in a field outside Gibeah, Jonathan warned David to flee. The parting was a difficult one with weeping and embracing. Probably both men wondered if their paths would ever cross again. But David was losing more than a friend. Running from Gibeah, he would lose his home, his wife and his esteemed military career in Saul's army. It is no wonder that the Bible records simply, "David wept the most" (20:41).

Jonathan said to David, "Go in peace, for we have sworn friendship with each other in the name of the LORD, saying, 'The LORD is witness between you and me, and between your descendants and my descendants forever'" (20:42). Then David left to take on the life of a fugitive. Jonathan returned to Gibeah to play out his role as the heir apparent.

Amazingly, the two men met again during a time when David must have been very discouraged. While on the run from Saul, David organized a ragged military gang. They lived by offering their services to beleaguered Israelite cities and farmers suffering attacks from the neighboring Philistines. Keilah was one such city. David and his men fought valiantly against the Philistines, defeating them and delivering the town to freedom. Word of David's victory spread quickly. Soon Saul set out afresh to capture him. When David learned Saul was on the march, he asked God whether the grateful citizens of Keilah would betray him, "And the LORD said, 'They will' " (23:12).

David and his army were forced to flee once more, this time to the arid wastes called the Desert of Ziph. When Saul learned David had left Keilah, he gave up pursuit. Yet a disheartening situation remained for David. He and his men had been betrayed by people whom should have gratefully offered them refuge, and Saul was still full of unjustified, murderous hatred toward him. The day that Samuel had anointed David as Israel's future king must have seemed like little more than a dream.

It was at this time that Jonathan again risked his father's wrath to meet with David. The Bible says simply, "And Saul's son Jonathan went to David at Horesh and helped him find strength in God" (23:16). This was the last time they met. Jonathan's words perfectly reflected God's design for Christian friendship: "Don't be afraid," Jonathan said. "My father Saul will not lay a hand on you. You will be king over Israel, and I will be second to you. Even my father Saul knows this"

(23:17). Sadly, Jonathan's picture of living under David's reign never came true because Jonathan died in battle before David took the throne.

The Power of a Triple Bond

Christian friendship carries life-changing power in several ways—all of which characterized the friendship of David and Jonathan. Notice Jonathan's continual efforts to focus their friendship on God. When David sought Jonathan's help in assessing Saul's murderous intentions, Jonathan strengthened his vow to David by calling on God as his witness five times (20:12-16). And when Jonathan visited David in the desert, his foremost purpose was to help David find strength in God. Their story exemplifies the verse from Ecclesiastes:

> Though one may be overpowered,
>   two can defend themselves.
> A cord of three strands is
>   not quickly boken.
>   (4:12)

Are the things of God at the core of your friendships? Is He the unseen, but welcome Guest during your times together, or would He be ashamed of your conversation? Jonathan kept God foremost in his time with David. To suggest that there was anything ungodly about the friendship between these two men is to overlook the holy God who bound them together. I believe that much of the reason David could later be described as a "man after God's own heart" was due to the influence of Jonathan.

Even as the son of King Saul, Jonathan couldn't solve all of David's dilemmas. Due to the political tensions of the day, they could rarely spend time together. But from the start Jonathan nurtured a triple bond of friendship—God, Jonathan and David. Jonathan knew that if something prevented him from being available for his friend, God would carry on. It was a strengthening insight David learned from Jonathan and one day set to music.

> You hem me in—behind and before;
> you have laid your hand upon me....
> How precious to me are your thoughts, O
> God!
> How vast is the sum of them!
> Were I to count them,
> they would outnumber the grains of
> sand.
> When I awake,
> I am still with you.
> (Psalm 139:5, 17-18)

We can't always be there for friends in times of need. But we can encourage each other to grow deeper in our walk with Christ.

Praying together is a simple way to begin stretching your friendship to include God.

Another suggestion is to attend Christian functions together or share with one another what God is doing in your life. If a spiritual focus is a mutual desire, praying and sharing about the things of God will deepen your friendship. It will also help your friend grow spiritually. And should life's circumstances part you, she'll take with her an empowering legacy in Christ.

The Power of Prophecy

Prophecy has gotten a bad rap over the years. This is mostly because we think of prophecy in the same terms as fortune-telling, like some mystical ability to foresee the future. But prophecy is also the ability to set forth a future. In fact, much of the Old Testament prophecy had to do with outlining the natural consequences of Israel's choices.

When we urge a friend onward to realize her full potential, we are being prophetic. Jonathan continually urged David on toward his God-given future. For example, consider Jonathan's gift of a royal robe and armor. Following David's victory over Goliath, his shepherd's garb was no longer appropriate. Jonathan focused David's eyes on the future by giving him the garb of a warrior and the robe of a king.

In his final words with David, Jonathan again helped his friend look past the present heartaches to the day when he would reign as king. He said, "You will be king over Israel, and

I will be second to you. Even my father Saul knows this" (1 Samuel 23:17). The fact that Jonathan would never see David crowned as king separates his words from literal prophecy. Yet without a doubt, the life-shaping blessing his words conveyed helped shape David to eventually rule as Israel's mightiest monarch.

Our friendships have incredible creative power. This is why Proverbs warns us to choose our friends wisely. We will be held back, or propelled ahead, by the company we keep.

Stepping out into a speaking and writing ministry has been an immense step of faith for me. I am sure this is the Lord's leading, but my convictions are often rocked by doubt and discouragement. It's at times like these that the prophetic words or actions of a friend have bolstered my fading initiative and helped me to keep going. Words like these have given me hope:

"I really believe God has gifted you in this area."

"I know the Lord is going to use this book to touch many lives."

"It will happen, it's just a matter of God's timing."

These verbal glimpses of a productive future under God's direction are powerful weapons against Satan's darts of doubt and fear.

Unfortunately, the opposite is also true. Words that reflect ridicule or doubt can stunt a person's potential faster than anything I know. Most of us recognize emotional abuse for the destructive power that it wields. But what about words like these?

"I don't know. I could never do that!"

"I don't want to tell you 'I told you so,' but it will never work."

"There's no way you'll make it. Why don't you just quit?"

Certainly urging a friend to attempt something she isn't suited for is equally destructive. If someone suggested that I pursue an accounting position, they wouldn't be doing anyone a favor. But such a suggestion may be appropriate for a friend with an affinity for math. Yet often we limit our friends by viewing life through our own filters of talents and disabilities. If we can't do it, we can't imagine that they could. Sometimes we may selfishly hold our friends back. After all, urging them to their God-designed potential may move them beyond the current comfortable relationship. Like David and Jonathan, our paths may ultimately lead in different directions. Or perhaps like Saul's relationship with David, we fear that our friend's success will be greater than our own.

If a person's identity is solidly grounded in Christ, then she can be the friend whom God intends for her to be. Because Jonathan saw his future secure in God's hands, he could selflessly support David's path to the throne. Only if we have attached ourselves to the kindred Spirit of Christ can we truly have the kindred hearts that God intends.

Sandy and I were the only two distance runners the year I ran in collegiate track. She was on the team first, had immeasurably more experience and actually recruited me. What's more, Sandy seemed almost tireless. Part of our regular workout required running up a steep quarter mile hill under a certain number of seconds. I hated this workout. Sandy didn't especially enjoy it either. Yet whenever we did it, she always used her rest time at the top to cheer for me. "Come on, Cheryl," she'd yell. "You can do it. I know you can! Come on, girl! Come on!"

The hill never became a favorite workout of mine, but I know I charged up it more often than if Sandy had never painted that verbal picture of accomplishment for me.

Then as the year progressed, an amazing thing happened. I became faster than Sandy, especially in the longer distance events. Still she never let her competitive edge run over our friendship. I didn't have to sacrifice our friendship to be my best. It was something I deeply respected in her.

Our kindred friendship shifted brightly in one race with a two mile event. Within a short time Sandy and I easily pulled to a large lead. By the time we hit a mile and a half we had actually lapped our competitors! Finally we rounded the last curve, the usual place for my final kick to the finish line. First place was unquestionably within my grasp. Then I did something that made no competitive sense, but made all kinds of relational sense. I moved over a lane, slowed a bit and stretched out my hand to Sandy. That day we crossed the finish line together hand-in-hand, both winners in more ways than one.

In his book, *The Blessing*, Gary Smalley writes:

> Words that picture a special future act like a campfire on a dark night. They can draw a person toward the warmth of genuine concern and fulfilled potential. Instead of leaving a child [or friend] to head into a dark unknown, they can illuminate a pathway lined with hope and purpose. (Smalley 1986, 89)

This is how God wants to use intimate Christian friendship. We are to be an inspiration to one another, selflessly urging each other on to be our personal best for God. Christ said it is our love for one another that is our testimony before the world. What begins here around the communion table extends into eternity. Christian friendship is both an awesome privilege and a tremendous blessing. Let God fill your life and transform your friendships. It is my prayer that you will settle for nothing less.

Making It Yours

1. A quote from this chapter reads: "I believe that much of the reason David could later be described as a 'man after God's own heart' was due to the godly influence of Jonathan." Do you agree or disagree with this statement? Explain your answer.

2. Barnabas means "son of encouragement." Read the story of Barnabas' friendship with Paul and John Mark.

   Paul's initial difficulties:
      Acts 9:21-26
   Barnabas' ministry to Paul:
      Acts 9:27, 11:19-26
   Paul's ministry:
      Acts 9:28-31, 11:25-30
   John Mark's initial difficulties:
      Acts 12:25 to 13:5,13
   Barnabas' ministry to John Mark:
      Acts 15:36-39
   Evidence of John Mark's ministry:
      Colossians 4:10, 2 Timothy 4:11

   How was Barnabas an encourager to each friend?

   Do you think Paul and John Mark's biographies read as success stories today partly due to Barnabas' ministry of encouragement? Why or why not?

3. Consider the story of another biblical friendship we often overlook. Read Second Kings 2:1-14.

   What was the legacy Elijah's friendship left to Elisha?

   What is the unique legacy that Christian friendship can offer another person?

4. Helping a friend picture the future God has for them is a powerful way Christians can empower one another. Read Mary's visit with Elizabeth in Luke 1:39-45.

   What difficulties and fears did Mary face in becoming the mother of Jesus? How might Elizabeth's greeting have encouraged Mary? How did Elizabeth's greeting picture God's future role for Mary?

5. Jesus pictured a future for His friends, especially the simple, impulsive, fisherman named Peter. Read Matthew 16:13-20. How might Jesus' words have encouraged Peter and helped shape his future?

6. What are two ways God has used this book to shape your thinking about Christian friendship? How do you plan to implement what you've learned?

Bibliography

Allender, Dan and Temper Longman III. *Bold Love*. Colorado Springs: Navpress, 1992.

Anderson, Neil T. *The Bondage Breaker*. Eugene, OR: Harvest House Publishers, 1990.

Arluke, Arnold and Jack Levin. *Gossip*. New York: Plenum Press, 1987.

Baldwin, Joyce G. *1 & 2 Samuel "An Introduction and Commentary."* Downers Grove, IL: Inter varsity Press, 1988.

Block, Joel D. *Friendship*. New York: MacMillian Publishing Co., 1980.

Brestin, Dee. *The Friendships of Women*. Wheaton, IL: Victor Books, 1988.

Briscoe, Stuart and Jill. *Pulling Together When You're Pulled Apart*. Wheaton, IL: Victor Books, 1991.

Byrne, Robert. *1,911 Best Things Anybody Ever Said.* New York: Fawcett Columbine [1984], 1988.

Christenson, Evelyn. *What Happens When Women Pray.* Wheaton, IL: Victor Books, 1975.

Clemens, Samuel L. *The Adventures of Huckleberry Finn.* New York: Dodd, Mead & Company, Inc. [originally published in 1885], 1984 edition.

DeAre, Diane. *"Geographical Mobility," Population Profile of the United States 1993.* U.S. Department of Commerce, Economics and Statistics Administration, Bureau of Census, 1993.

Eareckson Tada, Joni. *Choices Changes.* Grand Rapids, MI: Zondervan Books, 1986.

Ellison, Craig W. *Loneliness "The Search for Intimacy."* Chappaqua, New York: Christian Herald Books, 1980.

Fields, Doug. *Creative Romance.* Eugene, OR: Harvest House Publishers, 1991.

Focus on the Family Magazine. Vol. 18, Colorado Springs: Focus on the Family, March 1994.

Graves, Robert. *The Greek Myths. Vol. 1,* New York: Penguin Books, 1955.

Griffin, John Howard. *Black Like Me*. New York: Penguin Books [1960], 1976.

Katherine, Anne: *Boundaries "Where You End and I Begin."* Park Ridge, IL: Parkside Publishing Corp., 1991.

Kinder, Melvyn and Connell Cowan. *Husbands and Wives*. New York: Clarkson N. Potter, Inc., 1989.

Lerner, Harriet Goldhor. *The Dance of Intimacy*. New York: Harper & Row Publishers, Inc., 1989.

Lewis, C.S. *The Four Loves*. Orlando: Harcourt Brace Jovanovich, 1960.

Lockyer Sr., Herbert., ed. *Nelson's Illustrated Bible Dictionary*. Nashville: Thomas Nelson, Inc., Publishers, 1986.

Marshall, I. Howard. *The Acts of the Apostles "An Introduction and Commentary."* Grand Rapids: Wm. B. Eerdmans Publishing Co., 1980.

Miller, Joy Erlichman. *Addictive Relationships*. Deerfield Beach, FL: Health Communications, Inc., 1989.

Montgomery, L.M. *Anne of Green Gables*. New York: Bantam Books, 1908 (renewed 1935).

Montgomery, L.M. *Anne of Avonlea.* New York: Bantam Books, 1909 (renewed 1936).

Pennebaker, James W. *Opening Up.* New York: William Morrow and Company, Inc., 1990.

Saggs, H.W.F. *The Might That Was Assyria.* London: Sidgwick & Jackson Limited, 1984.

Schultz, Terri. *Bittersweet.* New York: Thomas Y. Crowell Company, 1976.

Shain, Merle. *When Lovers Are Friends.* New York: Bantam Books, 1978.

Smalley, Gary and John Trent. *The Blessing.* New York: Pocket Books, 1986.

The New Encyclopaedia Britannica "Macropaedia" Vol. 14, 15th edition, Chicago: Encyclopaedia Britannica, Inc., 1911-1990.

Thomas, Robert L., ed., *New American Standard Exhaustive Concordance of the Bible.* Nashville: Holman Bible Publishers, 1981.

Townsend, John and Henry Cloud. *Boundaries.* Grand Rapids: Zondervan Publishing House, 1992.

Vanauken, Sheldon. *A Severe Mercy.* New York: HarperCollins Publishers, Inc., 1977, 1980.

Vine, W.E. (Old Testament edited by F.F. Bruce) *Vine's Expository Dictionary of Old and New Testament Words.* Old Tappan, NJ: Fleming H. Revell Company, 1981.